Climate Mitigation and Carbon Finance

NIPA® GENX ELECTRONIC RESOURCES & SOLUTIONS P. LTD.
New Delhi-110 034

Climate Mitigation and Carbon Finance

Global Initiatives and Challenges

Dr. A.K. SAHOO
Assistant Professor
College of Forestry and CCPI, NAIP on Carbon Finance
Directorate of Research, Orissa University of Agriculture & Technology
Bhubaneswar-751 003 (Orissa) India

NIPA® GENX ELECTRONIC RESOURCES & SOLUTIONS P. LTD.
New Delhi-110 034

NIPA® GENX ELECTRONIC
RESOURCES & SOLUTIONS P. LTD.

101,103, Vikas Surya Plaza, CU Block
L.S.C. Market, Pitam Pura, New Delhi-110 034
Ph : +91 11 27341616, 27341717, 27341718
E-mail: newindiapublishingagency@gmail.com
www: www.nipabooks.com

For customer assistance, please contact
Phone: + 91-11-27 34 17 17
Fax: + 91-11- 27 34 16 16
E-Mail: feedbacks@nipabooks.com

ISBN: 978-81-19072-□0-7

Composed and Designed by NIPA®.

Prof. D.P. Ray
Vice Chancellor

visit us at : ouat.ac.in
Tel : (0674) 2397700 (O), 2561606 (R)
Fax : 91+674-2397780
E-mail : vcouat@indiatimes.com
ouat_dproy@yahoo.co.in
Orissa University of Agriculture & Technology
Bhubhaneswar-751003

Foreword

The Clean Development Mechanism (CDM) of Kyoto Protocol recognizes carbon sequestration as a way to mitigate global climate change and also allows industrialized countries to offset their carbon emissions by investing in forestry projects in developing countries. In addition, may private organizations, industries and corporate bodies are promoting carbon sequestration projects to reduce their carbon emissions. The economic and environmental benefits of carbon sequestration projects are particularly relevant for India, which need increased investment to arrest forest degradation and poverty alleviation. With a high dependence on land and forests for subsistence, india requires effective strategies to combat the growing threat of natural resource degradation, and to meet the demand for biomass from forests as well. Many natural resource management projects become unviable, either because their environmental services were uncompensated or because state governments and other local agencies do not have adequate funds to undertake conservation activities. Carbon sequestration projects can address both these concerns by paying for some of the services (such as carbon sequestration) and by providing financial assistance to local communities to invest in natural resource projects with a view to abate GHG emissions while providing income opportunities for communities. Such a forestry practice would significantly contribute in carbon sequestration and improve socio-economic condition of the people. In addition, it can conserve biodiversity by reducing large scale removals of fuel-wood from natural forests, and also provide livelihood options in rural areas, which can curb poverty driven forest degradation. Carbon finance benefits under the framework of Kyoto Protocol of UNFCCC increase the value of forests relative to other land uses. So, CDM forestry projects can definitely provide a strong impetus to serve as an effective strategy for biodiversity conservation challenges and also supplement state and national policy efforts to address such a global issue of climate change.

I appreciate the endeavours of Dr. A.K. Sahoo in bringing out a book on "Climate Mitigation and Carbon Finance " encompassing with all these aspects. The book not only reviews the existing scientific and policy literatures on the global issue of climate change but also provides an insight into the gap in the carbon financing procedure under Kyoto mechanisms of UNFCCC. I hope this book will be very much useful for teachers, researchers, policy makers, validators, students, beneficiaries and all those interested in carbon finance.

10 May, 2011 (Prof. D.P. Ray)

Preface

Climate change over the years has gained a wide recognition in scientific community and is now considered an imminent threat. To help deal with this, the international community created the Kyoto Protocol to the United Nations Framework Convention on Climate Change (UNFCCC), under which emission-reduction targets were set for developed countries (so-called Annex-1 countries) and policy mechanisms devised to help countries to meet these targets through carbon sequestration in different sectors. The CDM is one such mechanism of Kyoto protocol that took shape in 2005 and allows various kinds of emission reduction projects, of which afforestation and reforestation (A/R) projects are of interest to the forest sector.

India with its myriad opportunities for afforestation/ reforestation at both National and local scale holds a special prospect in this context. As a developing country, India possesses a huge market for investments by the developed economies in order to fulfill their emission targets. The Kyoto Protocol may provide an opportunity for rural community to uplift their livelihoods by carbon forestry and by linking to carbon trading markets. Clean Development Mechanism (CDM) projects in India needs to focus on small holders, who do sequester carbon and also reduce emissions through their plantations, individually as well as collectively, and hence should qualify for the minimum tradable carbon. The economic value of forestry carbon needs to be assessed with consideration for both onsite and offsite effects. Further the priority focus need to shift policies which can facilitate financial incentives for net carbon sequestration at the local scale. Fostering linkages between carbon trading markets and the local carbon sequestration efforts is an essentiality in streamlining the entire mechanism in economic terms. In India, since beginning Government has treated CDM as a mechanism targeted mostly at the private sector, and facilitated its growth through capacity building initiatives and the issuance of clear and transparent rules for project approval. India was the second largest supplier of emission reductions in 2006 (by volume of emission reduction sold) at 12% of all CDM transactions, behind China at 61%. It is thus evident that India is being outperformed by China with the main reasons being the average project size (China has twice the average size than India), and notable absence of both the public sector and the financial players from India. There is a significant knowledge gap in understanding the potential of A/R projects in the Indian scenario. Moreover, it is essential for project developers to get full access to relevant for the design of project activities.

This book is thus an attempt to make the readers fully realize the potential of A/R-CDM to deliver resources for the rehabilitation of degraded lands and the sustainable development of non annex countries. The comprehensive view by the book on Clean Development Mechanism and Carbon Markets in relation to forestry projects would help in developing the faculty on growing importance and need of forestry activities as emission reduction measures.

The author is extremely thankful to Dr.V.P Singh, Regional Representative, World Agroforestry Centre (ICRAF), South-Asia, New Delhi for his sincere support and academic encouragement. His scientific inputs and critical assessment gave a strong base for developing such a publication of its kind. The author is also extremely thankful to Prof.D.P.Ray, Vice-Chancellor, Orissa University of Agriculture and Technology for his constant support and moral encouragement. The author also gratefully acknowledges the support rendered by PIU, NAIP in bringing this issue to a book form and help a number of users and beneficiaries to avail the benefit of carbon finance. The author gratefully acknowledges Dr.R.K.Patnaik, Dean, College of Forestry and Dr. M. Panda, Dean of Research, OUAT, Bhubaneswar for their support and sincere cooperation. Further, the author is also thankful to the publisher for bringing out this edition with success.

May, 2011 **A.K. SAHOO**

Acronyms and Abbreviations

AAA	Analytical and Advisory Activity
AAU	Assigned Amount Unit
AFOLU	Agriculture and Forestry Land Use
A/R	Afforestation/Reforestation
ARD	Afforestation, Reforestation and Deforestation
AWG	Adhoc Working Group
AIJ	Activities Implemented Jointly
BEE	Bureau of Energy Efficiency
BERM	Brazilian Emission Reduction Market
BioCF	Biocarbon Fund
BM&F	Brazilian Mercantile and Future Exchange
CAR	Corrective Action Request
CCB	Climate, Community and Biodiversity
CCX	Chicago Climate Exchange
CDCF	Community Development Carbon Fund
CDM	Clean Development Mechanism
CER	Certified Emission Reduction
CFL	Compact Fluorescent Lamp
CLRs	Clarification Requests
COP	Conference of Parties
DCF	Danish Carbon Fund

DOE	Designated Operational Entity
DNA	Designated National Authority
EB-CDM	Executive Board of the Clean Development Mechanism
ER	Emission Reduction
EU	European Union
EU- ETS	European Union Emissions Trading Scheme
EUA	European Union Allowances
FAO	Food and Agriculture Organisation
FCPF	Forest Carbon Partnership Facility
FMC	Forward Market Commission
GHGs	Green House Gas Emissions
GoI	Government of India
GPS	Global Positioning System
GWP	Global Warming Potential
ICF	Italian Carbon Fund
ICRAF	International Centre for Research in Agroforestry
IET	International Emissions Trading
IFAP	International Federation of Agriculture Producers
IJI	Initiative on Joint Implementation
IPCC	Inter-governmental Panel on Climate Change
IRR	Internal Rate of Return
JBIC	Japan Bank for International Cooperation
JI	Joint Implementation
LoA	Letter of Approval
LDCs	Least Developed Countries
LULUCF	Land Use, Land Use Change and Forestry
LCER	Long Term Certified Emission Reduction

MCEoI	Multi Commodity Exchange of India
MoEF	Ministry of Environment and Forests
MOP	Meeting of the Parties
MOU	Memorandum of Understanding
MUD	Ministry of Urban Development
NCDF	Netherland Clean Development Facility
NCDE	National Commodities and Derivatives Exchange
NECF	Netherland European Carbon facility
ODA	Official Development Assistance
PDD	Project Design Document
PoA	Program of Activities
PIN	Project Idea Note
PSUs	Public Sector Units
REDD	Reducing Emissions from Deforestation and Degradation
SCF	Spanish Carbon Fund
SEBI	Securities and Exchange Board of India
SOA	Standard Operating Procedure
SMEs	Small and Medium Enterprises
tCER	Temporary Certified Emission Reduction
UNFCCC	United Nations Framework Convention on Climate Change
UNEP	United Nations Environment Program
VER	Verified Emission Reduction

❑❑❑

Contents

Chapter-1

CDM Afforestation and Reforestation Project

1.1 Policy Background

Human activities have resulted in the alteration of the composition of our atmosphere triggering change in the Earth's climate. The world's population has grown at an alarming rate with a corresponding increase in demand for natural resources, energy, food, and goods. As a consequence of increase in consumption, vast quantities of gases and effluents are discharged that change the composition of the atmosphere and its capacity to regulate its temperature. The rise in the global temperature is caused by the accumulation of the so-called "greenhouse gases", namely, carbon dioxide (CO_2), methane, nitrous oxide, and chlorofluorocarbons. Energy received from the sun is absorbed as short wavelength radiation and is eventually returned to space as long wavelength infrared radiation. Greenhouse gases absorb the infrared radiation, trapping it in the atmosphere in the form of heat energy. By increasing the atmosphere's ability to absorb infrared energy, the greenhouse gases are disturbing the way the climate maintains the balance between incoming and outgoing energy (UNFCCC 2001). This increases the probability of occurrence of unseen and unpredictable events across the planet. There has been an increase of average global surface temperature by 0.6°C during the last 100 years as a consequence of human activities, such as deforestation and burning of fossil fuels. The Intergovernmental Panel on Climate Change (IPCC 2001) stated in its Third Assessment Report that the globally averaged surface temperature is projected to increase by 1.4°C to 5.8°C from 1990 to 2100 under business-as-usual, and sea levels by 9 cm to 88 cm over the same period. If nothing is done to prevent or limit these changes, they will have major consequences for the ecosystem. The effects of climate change are manifested in several ways globally, precipitation is on the rise. In the northern hemisphere, precipitation has increased by 0.5% to 1.0% per decade whereas the increase in tropical countries has been 0.2% to 0.3% per decade. The changes in the global climate have caused a reduction of the snow pack in northern latitudes, a melting of mountain glaciers, a thawing of the arctic permafrost, and a shrinking of the polar ice caps. The average sea level of the world's oceans has risen 10 cm to 20 cm in the last century. UNEP models 2002 predict an increase in global mean sea level of between 13 cm and 94 cm by the year 2100; however, other models predict a sea level rise by 54cm to 68 cm by 2100.These consequences will include geographic shifts in the occurrence of different species and/or the extinction of species. Changes in rainfall patterns will put pressure on water resources in many regions, which will, in turn, affect both irrigation and drinking water supplies. Extreme weather events and floods will become more frequent with their increasing economic costs and human suffering. River deltas that are presently being farmed and estuaries that are now important wildlife habitats will be flooded and become saline, making them unsuitable for these uses. Warm seasons will become dryer in the interior of most mid-latitude continents, increasing the frequency of droughts and land degradation. This will be particularly serious for areas where land degradation, desertification and droughts are already severe. Additionally, tropical diseases will extend beyond their present geographic range. Developing countries would bear the maximum brunt of global warming and climate change the socioeconomic impact of climate change in developing countries will be significant. Rising temperatures and irregular precipitation patterns will impact negatively on agricultural crop yields, food security, and health issues related to malnutrition. An increased incidence and intensity of violent storms and monsoons will produce more flooding which, in turn, will cause greater damage to infrastructure and an increase in the incidence of vector-borne (e.g., malaria) and water-borne (e.g. cholera) diseases. The least privileged in society are also the least equipped to adapt to climate change. Human poverty, limited infrastructure, poor access to technology, inadequate education, and limited management skills; combine to frustrate the ability of developing countries to respond to the challenges.

The developing countries will bear the maximum brunt of global warming and climate change, although their contribution to greenhouse gas emissions is much less than that of the developed countries. It is, therefore, important that countries like India take proactive steps to contribute to fighting climate change. The forestry sector has the potential to sequester carbon. However, managing natural forests alone for maximizing carbon sequestration will compromise with other ecological functions of natural forests. Hence, the need for policy support for carbon mitigation mechanism such as production forestry/ agro-forestry carried out outside the natural forest area for meeting the demand of fuel wood and timber of the country. Production forestry in India can not only bridge the constantly increasing gap between demand and supply of industrial timber but also help the nation enhance carbon sequestration. In addition, it can help conserve bio-diversity by reducing large-scale fuel wood removals from natural forest areas and create much needed alternative employment opportunities in rural areas to curtail poverty driven forest degradation. The present government policies are to be fine-tuned in order to make them conducive to the growth of production forestry to its fullest potential. It is, therefore, necessary to create a better understanding of the potential of production forestry in carbon mitigation in India, analyze the policy and procedural constraints that hinder the achievement of this potential and increase the level of awareness of policy makers about the importance of enhancing country's wood production outside natural forest areas.

In 1992, most countries joined the United Nations Framework Convention on Climate Change (UNFCCC) to begin considering what could be done to reduce global warming and how to cope with whatever temperature increases might result. A major accomplishment of the Convention, which is general and flexible in character, is that it, recognised there was a problem, a significant accomplishment in 1994 when the UNFCCC was ratified by 189 countries, because at that time less scientific evidence was available.

The UNFCCC sets an ultimate objective of stabilizing greenhouse gas emissions "at a level that would prevent dangerous anthropogenic (human induced) interference with the climate system". It states that "such a level should be achieved within a time-frame sufficient to allow ecosystems to adapt naturally to climate change, to ensure that food production is not threatened, and to enable economic development to proceed in a sustainable manner".

Countries that have ratified the UNFCCC called "Parties to the Convention" agree to take climate change into account in matters such as agriculture, industry, energy, natural resources and activities involving sea coasts. They have also agreed to develop national programmes to slow climate change on a voluntary basis. The Convention places the heaviest burden for halting climate change on industrialised nations because they are the source of most past and current greenhouse gas emissions.

The first step in solving a problem is to know its dimensions. To address this issue, the Parties of the "developed nations" and nations with "economies in transition" (called Annex I countries because they are listed in the first annex to the Convention) are required to report updated inventories of greenhouse gas emissions on a regular basis. With a few exceptions, the "base year" for tabulating greenhouse gas emissions has been set as 1990.

Developing countries (also referred to as non-Annex I countries) also are encouraged to compile greenhouse gas inventories. The UNFCCC is recognised as a "framework" document - that is, something to be amended or augmented over time so that efforts to deal with global warming and climate change can be focused and made more effective. The first addition to the Convention, the Kyoto Protocol, which contains more powerful (and legally binding) measures, was adopted in 1997.

The challenge is to implement policies and programs that can respond to development priorities, which at the same time help to reduce vulnerability to poverty and climate change, limit emissions, and increase carbon sinks (Garrity, 2009, Patnaik & Sahoo, 2009 and Roshetko *et.al* 2006). One of the production technologies that is affordable and reasonably meets these important criteria is land use practices based on agroforestry and conservation agriculture principles. Although agroforestry systems in providing multiple benefits are widely recognized, the specifics of how these systems can best be implemented are generally misunderstood, or inappropriately applied in many ambitious investment projects.

In general, this protocol advocates a gradual transition and transformation of "field crop agriculture" based livelihood systems to agroforestry based livelihood systems, including the field crops, and promotes the adoption of the emission reducing interventions in the farming- house hold operations. The agroforestry based systems have been documented to provide an insulation effect from climatic vagaries to the farming and at the same time sequester significant amount of carbon, both in the above and the below ground biomass. A recent UNFCC report (UNFCC, 2008) has concluded that the carbon sequestration in grasslands and agroforestry plantations have significant potential for C reductions from the agriculture sector at non-prohibitive costs'. Beyond mitigating climate change, the other benefits of having trees on the landscape include the maintenance and improvement of soil productivity, biodiversity and ecosystem services, many of which are highly correlated with the carbon stocks in soil and biomass.

1.2 The Kyoto Protocol

Under the UNFCCC, Parties agreed to annual meetings called Conferences of the Parties (COP 2). At the Third COP in Kyoto, Japan, in 1997, a protocol was agreed that set greenhouse gas emission reduction targets for industrialised countries and countries with economies in transition. Annex I countries committed to reducing their emissions by an average of 5 percent below 1990 levels in the period 2008-2012. The Kyoto Protocol came into force on the 16 February 2005. To date, 163 states have ratified (or acceded to) the Kyoto Protocol, including 35 Annex I countries (whose emissions represent 61.6 percent of total Annex I Party emissions).

The Kyoto Protocol of the United Nations Framework Convention on Climate Change (UNFCCC) initiates the international efforts to reduce the GHG emissions and address climate change (IPCC, 2000, 2001 and 2007; UNFCCC, 1996, 2000,2001; FAO, 2004, Sahoo *et.al* 2010, Sahoo, 2011 and Sahoo *et. al* 2011). The said protocol envisaged binding commitments of GHG reductions for developed countries by an average of 5 % relative to 1990 levels by 2008-12. As a result, carbon offset has become a tradable commodity. Forests and agricultural crops and soils can remove and store carbon dioxide from the atmosphere. These carbon sequestration activities are called 'sinks'. Sinks can be enhanced through sustainable management practices in forestry and on farms. The Kyoto Protocol provides for inclusion of sinks as part of a country's strategy to meet its obligations. India signed and ratified the Protocol in August 2002. Since India is exempted from the framework of the Treaty, it is expected to gain from the Protocol in terms of transfer of technology and related foreign investments. Another important feature of this is the fast growth nature of trees, which could enable the practice to easily respond to climate change. Carbon sequestration is considered as one of the important strategies under Kyoto protocol, through sink enhancement. The Kyoto Protocol potentially offers an opportunity for capital investment and technology transfer for commercial forestry, under the afforestation/reforestation activities of the Clean Development Mechanism (CDM).Carbon sequestration through sink enhancement by way of growing more trees is one of the cost-effective modes of achieving this objective (Noble and Scholes, 2001). Industrialized countries are allowed to buy carbon credits developed by carbon sequestration projects through Land-Use, Land-Use Change and Forestry (LULUCF) options in developing countries. Under the Kyoto Protocol, Annex I countries need to invest under LULUCF activities while determining their net GHG emissions under allowed allowances (Kennett, 2002) .It gives the industries, targeted for emitting GHGs the flexibility to continue using fossil fuels for some time, which will act as a buffer in the process of switching over to more efficient energy source, if they invest in sequestering carbon. It would help to achieve the goal of sustainable development throughout the world by bringing investment from developed world to developing countries. CDM projects in India could also lead to a large positive impact on programmes aimed at forest conservation and regeneration, reclamation of degraded land and socio-economic development of rural communities in addition to global environmental benefits.

The investment by developed countries would enhance the rate of afforestation/reforestation and other additional activities to meet the biomass needs and reclaim degraded and wastelands in the country. Now this is being looked upon as a major benefit with market instruments favoring the active involvement of industry in the mechanism. The potential of India is quite high for CDM related projects. Although it is not mandatory for Indian industries to meet any sort of targets under Kyoto, they still prefer to favour this phenomenon as it strengthens their claim over wastelands of the country. Further, farmers are known to be the most efficient producers of sequestered carbon, stored in trees grown for fruits, timber and other tree products, as well as reduced emissions by adopting the conservation agricultural practices in the farming (Verchot, 2009 and Singh, 2009). Theses are approximately 1.5 billion ha of arable farmlands in the developing countries that are suitable for conversion to highly productive carbon rich agroforestry landscapes that can at the same-time contribute to food security, income generation and yet sequester substantial amounts of carbon in sinks (Garrity, 2009; Garrity, *et al,* 2008).

Three market-based "flexible mechanisms" were included under the Kyoto Protocol to help reduce the cost of implementation. These mechanisms allow industrialised countries to reduce emissions outside their national boundaries and to count these reductions towards their national target. The mechanisms are:

- International Emissions Trading (Article 17), which allows Annex I Parties to trade part of their assigned cap;
- Joint Implementation (Article 6), which functions at the sub-national level so that project activities can be sponsored and implemented in one Annex I country to meet reduction requirements in a second Annex I country; and
- The Clean Development Mechanism (Article 12), which allows the sponsorship and implementation of project activities in non-Annex I Parties and is the focus of this book.

1.3 Clean Development Mechanism (CDM)

The CDM, like Joint Implementation, is a project-based mechanism. However, unlike Joint Implementation and International Emissions Trading, the CDM involves host Parties that do not themselves have an emissions cap or emissions reduction target. The CDM, as detailed under Article 12 of the Protocol, states:

"The purpose of the clean development mechanism shall be to assist ... [non-Annex I Parties] ... in achieving sustainable development and ... to assist ... [Annex I Parties] in achieving compliance with their quantified ... commitments ..."

A CDM project activity is undertaken at a specific location in a non-Annex I host country where CDM finances or the prospect of CDM financing leads to either a reduction in emissions or an increase in sequestration. The difference in quantity of emissions or sequestrations between what occurs with the project and what would have occurred without the project is tradable. Once verified, this difference becomes x tonnes of Certified Emissions Reductions (or CERs, the CDM trading unit) which, when purchased by an Annex I Party, is

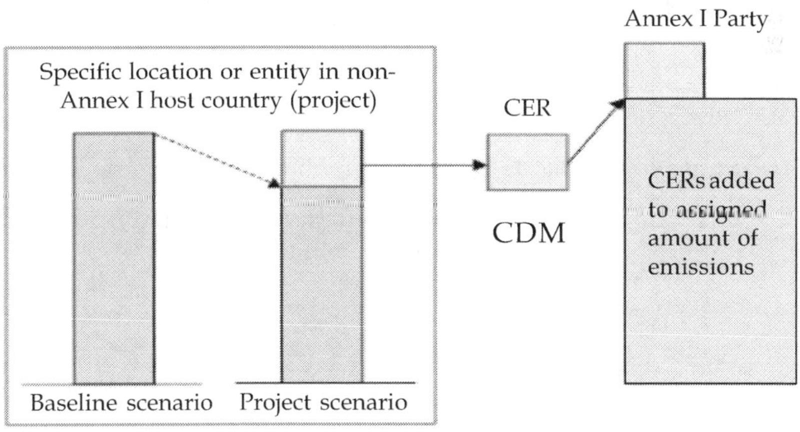

Fig. 1: The Baseline and Project Scenario

added to that Party's assigned emissions and permits the Annex I Party to emit an additional quantity of carbon dioxide (CO_2) or non-CO_2 gases equal to the verified CER.

As trading under the CDM takes place with non-capped hosts, the CDM leads to an increase in the total amount of the emissions cap of Annex I countries. The CDM effectively grants a license to emit up to the total emissions savings secured by project activities in non-Annex I host countries - that is, countries are trading emission offsets. The CDM, as its name implies, is supposed to stimulate clean development for the populations of non-Annex I countries.

There are 15 categories of eligible CDM project activities:

1. Energy industries (renewable/non-renewable sources);
2. Energy distribution;
3. Energy demand;
4. Manufacturing industries;
5. Chemical industries;
6. Construction;
7. Transport;
8. Mining/mineral production;
9. Metal production;
10. Fugitive emissions from fuels (solid, oil and gas);
11. Fugitive emissions from production and consumption of halocarbons and sulphur hexafluoride;
12. Solvent use;
13. Waste handling and disposal;
14. Afforestation and reforestation; and
15. Agriculture.

The CDM has two stated aims: to assist industrialized countries to meet their emission reduction targets by purchasing or generating carbon offsets and to support sustainable development in host countries (Kyoto Protocol Article 12.2). In other words, the CDM allows industrialized countries to meet a portion of their emission reduction targets by either purchasing carbon offsets that were generated through CDM-registered projects or earning carbon offsets by creating or investing in CDM-registered projects. While the CDM recognizes several activities that create carbon offsets, all CDM project activities must take place in and contribute to the sustainable development goals of non-Annex I (host) countries. This geographic restriction and the focus on sustainable development differentiate CDM activities from JI and other carbon-market activities that produce or accept different types of carbon offsets. Carbon offsets generated through all CDM project activities are known as Certified Emission Reductions (CERs) and are equivalent to one metric tonne of carbon dioxide.5 Within the CDM, afforestation and reforestation are the only Land Use, Land-Use Change and Forestry (LULUCF) activities (as designated in Article 3.3 of the Kyoto Protocol) recognized to create CERs .However, a post-2012 climate agreement is likely to change the CDM, broaden the activities recognized in the LULUCF classification or add new classifications that include activities such as agriculture, forestry or other land uses (AFOLU) and reduced emissions from deforestation and forest degradation (REDD+). The potential of CDM A/R projects to sequester carbon and to contribute to sustainable development is widely recognized. Yet, there are diverging opinions regarding whether such projects can be implemented worldwide, how 'sustainable development' can and should be defined ,whether market mechanisms actually contribute to carbon mitigation and whether benefits from carbon forestry projects, in general, and CDM A/R projects, in particular, are equitably distributed. Indeed, problems with the design, cost efficiencies and implementation of potential CDM A/R projects have effectively limited the number of afforestation and reforestation projects certified by the CDM. For example, of the nearly 1400 registered CDM projects, in early January 2009, there was only one A/R project - the Facilitating Reforestation for Guangxi Watershed Management in Pearl River Basin project in China. However, by May 2010, the number of registered CDM A/R projects had rapidly grown to 14 (out of 2171 total registered CDM projects) and there were 41 more CDM A/R projects requesting registration, under review, or at validation. It is estimated that if all these 41 applicants are registered, these 55 A/R projects will produce 15,780 (0.6%) of the 2,854,824 CERs expected to be generated by all CDM projects by 2012. Taken alone, the 14 currently registered CDM A/R projects should capture some 8084 kilotonnes of carbon dioxide by 2020. While the limited but quantifiable carbon sequestration of CDM A/R projects can be estimated, there are less data and less understanding of CDM A/R activities' socioeconomic impacts. As a result, analyses of these projects' impacts on sustainable development have been limited to hypothetical scenarios or to examinations of how prototype projects have functioned on the ground. Indeed, many articles that discuss the potential socioeconomic impacts of CDM A/R projects draw conclusions from case studies of voluntary forest carbon projects' and forest conservation projects' impacts on sustainable development. Yet, CDM A/R projects have a number of procedural requirements and unique institutional arrangements that might produce very different results from non-CDM projects.

1.3.1 Afforestation and Reforestation Projects under the CDM

A CDM project is an activity undertaken in a non-Annex I country that results in reduced emissions of greenhouse gases or increased sequestration. In the case of forestry projects, growing trees fix (or sequestrate) CO_2 from the atmosphere into stable living material. CDM projects must be registered with the Executive Board of the CDM. This is achieved through the validation of a Project Design Document by an official auditing organisation known as a Designated Operational Entity.

To prove there is an atmospheric benefit to a project activity, it is necessary to show the project is doing more than "business as usual" - in the case of afforestation and reforestation projects, increasing sequestration above that which was occurring before the start of project activities. The project must also be "additional", which means there must be certainty that the activity would not have occurred without the CDM incentive - that is, that CDM money was the critical catalyst. Finally, the project must also not lead to a displacement of emissions or "leakage", which would lead to a loss of the greenhouse gas benefits of the activity.

1.3.2 Relevant Afforestation and Reforestation Activities under the CDM

Despite the limitations to afforestation and reforestation, LULUCF project activities can still be relatively diverse and cover activities such as:

- Native forest restoration;
- Timber plantations;
- Agro forests/multi-purpose trees; and
- Recuperation of barren areas.

1.3.3 CDM Afforestation and Reforestation Project Rules and Conditions

CDM projects must result in carbon credits that are effectively permanent, in addition to business as usual, and will not lead to carbon losses outside the project boundaries.

1.3.3.1 Approach for addressing non-permanence

During the negotiations leading up to the Kyoto Protocol and subsequently, there was considerable concern that credits issued for carbon sequestration would be subject to a risk of re-emission due to either human action or natural events such as wildfires. This was called the permanence risk and is unique to LULUCF projects under the Protocol. The danger is that CO_2 removed from the atmosphere by trees will be re-released if the trees are cut down or fall in severe storms, or are burned by humans or in wildfires. To solve this concern, the Parties agreed at the Ninth COP (COP-9) that credits arising from afforestation/reforestation projects under the CDM should only be temporary. Although the credits are temporary, it was determined that they could be re-issued or renewed (every five years) after an independent verification deems that sufficient carbon is still sequestered within a project to account for all the credits issued.

Credit for CDM projects is given in the form of CERs. There are two forms of CERs: temporary (tCERs) and long-term (lCERs). Both types of credits basically view carbon sequestration as providing an ecosystem service that can be rented or leased over different time periods. A "tCER is a CER issued for an afforestation or reforestation project activity under the CDM, which expires at the end of the commitment period following the one during which it was issued". For example, a tCER issued at some point in the commitment period 2013-2017 would expire at the end of the next commitment period, 2022. At this time, the tCER can be reissued (if verification has occurred) either to the same Annex I buyer or another buyer. The Annex I buyer must replace the expired tCER with either a tCER or with a credit from another mechanism. At the end of the crediting period, all tCERs expire.An "lCER is a CER issued for an afforestation or reforestation project activity under the CDM, which expires at the end of the crediting period of the afforestation or reforestation project activity under the CDM for which it was issued". It is theoretically good for up to 20 to 30 years. lCERs must be replaced as soon as verification shows that the carbon stock has decreased, or if no verification has occurred for a period of five years. At the end of the crediting period, all lCERs expire. lCERs have variable expiration periods - for example, an lCER sold in year five of a 30-year project will have a duration of 25 years, while an lCER sold in year 10 of a 30- year project will have a duration of 20 years.

1.3.3.2 Leakage

Although projects will most likely successfully sequester carbon within the project area, some projects may alter activities or behaviours elsewhere. These activities may lead to reduced sequestration or increased emissions outside the project boundary, thus negating a portion of the benefits of the project. This is called leakage.

Two types of leakage are generally recognised: that caused by activity shifting and that caused by market effects. A simple example of leakage from activity shifting is a project that reforests poor-quality grazing land, but leads owners of the displaced livestock to clear land outside the project boundaries to establish new pastures. An example of leakage caused by market effects is a project that reforests large tracts of productive beef cattle grazing land. The reduction in supply of beef signals the market, causing prices to increase, and land is cleared elsewhere for producing more beef. Most projects under the CDM are unlikely to cause leakage from market effects. Activities that might result in leakage vary with the type of projects both LULUCF and non-LULUCF projects are subject to leakage. Leakage can often be minimised by good project design - for example, by including improved pasture management around a new forest so that displaced livestock can be accommodated without further clearing.

AR-NM0019 (the number assigned to this project by the CDM Executive Board) allows for the calculation of leakage from displacement of agricultural activities, livestock and fuel wood, vehicle use, and increased use of fence posts. The method for assessing the impact of displacement of agricultural activities involves tracking a proportion of the people displaced in the five years immediately after displacement. It is necessary to track what area each person deforests (if any). If the sampled people leave the area, then a conservative deforestation estimate is applied. For leakage through the displacement of livestock, it is necessary to track numbers of livestock for the first five years after displacement. Leakage is estimated from decreases in numbers of livestock within the project boundary after the start of project activities, in combination with an ex-ante calculation of the required grassland area per head of livestock. Leakage due to the displacement of fuel-wood collection is estimated through the average volume collected in the project area before the start of project activities, minus the volume collected within the boundaries after activity displacement.

For leakage due to fossil fuel use, the methodology requires tracking of distance traveled by project vehicles outside the project boundaries. Leakage is calculated by applying constants for fuel consumption and fuel emission factors. Leakage due to the increased use of fence posts compares the perimeter of fencing before and after project commencement. Total leakage is equal to the sum of each of the leakage components. Individual forms of leakage can be excluded and not monitored if it can reasonably be shown that the project will have no influence or will lead to a decrease in emissions.

1.3.3.3 Baseline

Afforestation/reforestation CDM projects enhance greenhouse gas removals in one country to permit an equivalent quantity of greenhouse gas emissions in another country, without changing the global emission balance. Technically, the CDM is a baseline-and-credit trade mechanism, not a cap-and-trade mechanism. Therefore, enhancements of removals by afforestation/ reforestation projects must create real, measurable and long term benefits related to the mitigation of climate change (Kyoto Protocol, Article 12.5b), and must be additional to any that would occur in the absence of the certified project activity (Article 12.5c). The in-the-absence scenario is also referred to as the baseline or 'business-as-usual' scenario. The purpose of baseline analysis is to provide a transparent picture of what would have happened in the absence of the proposed project.

A baseline scenario must be derived using a baseline methodology approved by the CDM Executive Board. The scenario should be established in a transparent and conservative manner regarding the choices of approaches and assumptions. Every single project should define its own baseline. In summary, the baseline must be the most likely course of action and development over time, in the absence of CDM financing.

As an example, the project scenario for most afforestation/ reforestation projects will be planting and maintaining trees that grow into forest. The baseline may be the low carbon stocks present in croplands or grazing lands, each of which will be constant through time. Equally, however, the baseline could be the abandonment of the land and subsequent natural

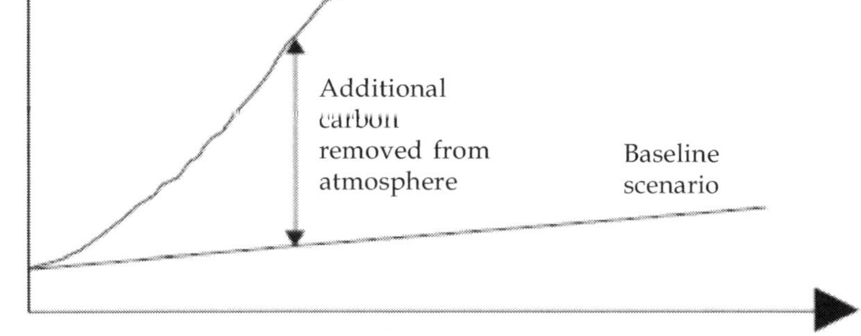

Fig. 2 : Time-path of carbon stocks in the project and the baseline scenarios.

regeneration of trees. In this case, the additional carbon removed from the atmosphere is equal to the difference between naturally regenerating and planted trees. The figure below shows the time-path of carbon stocks in the project and the baseline scenarios.

The baseline scenario can either be estimated and validated upfront, and then "frozen" for the first phase of the crediting period (30 years, or the first 20 years of a 60-year project), or it can be monitored during the afforestation/reforestation project. However, even in the latter case, it is still necessary to establish a methodology upfront on how to select the control plots and monitor them and it is also still necessary to provide an upfront estimation of the baseline, including the associated emissions and removals of greenhouse gases (although this upfront estimation is then only for information and not used for calculating emission reductions - the results of the monitored baseline would be used). The advantage of an upfront, estimated and "frozen" baseline is that there is greater certainty about the emission reductions generated by the project. This is the option that has been used by most projects to date and all currently approved methodologies (as of June 2006) assume baseline scenarios "frozen" during the crediting period.

Examples of baseline and project scenarios

1. San Nicolás CDM Afforestation Project

   Country: Colombia

   Project area: 8,730 hectares

   Baseline scenario: Abandoned pastures with no current economic use and so no possibility for displacement

   Baseline carbon stock: The stock of carbon in the pastures

   Project: Forest and agroforestry plantations

   Pico Bonito National Park Reforestation

   Country: Honduras

Project area: 2,600 hectares

Baseline scenario: Shifting agriculture

Baseline carbon stock: Conservatively estimated as the maximum stock recorded over the shifting agriculture cycle

Project: Reforestation with commercial plantations and natural forest restoration

1.3.3.4 Additionality

The CDM is a carbon-neutral process. It allows an Annex I country and a non Annex I country to co-operate on carrying out a project in the non-Annex I country that will sequester carbon (or reduce emissions). CERs are created through this project and transferred to the Annex I country, which is now able to emit an equivalent number of units of carbon while meeting its targets. Thus, the atmospheric concentration of greenhouse gases remains unchanged as a result of the transaction. The Annex I country is assisted in meeting its commitments cost effectively and, in well-designed projects, the non-Annex I country benefits in meeting its sustainable development goals. If a potential project that sequesters carbon (or reduces emissions) would have taken place without the CDM transaction, then the emission reductions are not additional and the greenhouse gases in the atmosphere would increase as a result of the transfer of CERs5. For example, if an area would have been reforested either through deliberate management action or natural processes, irrespective of the CDM transaction, then if the CDM transaction was erroneously allowed to take place the Annex I country would emit more greenhouse gases and the atmosphere will have a higher level of greenhouse gases than it would have without the transaction. The purpose of the additionality clause in Article 12 of the Kyoto Protocol is to prevent this from occurring.

Some confusion has arisen because the definition of additionality, as agreed to, does not fully capture the core concepts. The definition agreed to at the Ninth COP (COP- 9) in 2003 is: "The proposed afforestation or reforestation project activity under the CDM is additional if the actual net greenhouse gas removals by sinks are increased above the sum of the changes in carbon stocks in the carbon pools within the project boundary that would have occurred in the absence of the registered CDM afforestation or reforestation project activity...", which focuses more on identifying the additional component than on the project eligibility. It must be clear that additionality is not the difference between the baseline and project greenhouse gas emissions. Further guidance from the CDM Executive Board, and the recommended steps in dealing with additionality and baselines, is outlined in next chapter, including an additionality test devised by the Executive Board.

The essential question that must be asked of each project is: What quantity of carbon is being sequestered as a direct result of the CDM transaction, in anticipation of selling carbon offsets? Only this quantity of CERs can be issued. This test applies equally to LULUCF and non-LULUCF projects.

1.3.3.5 Land eligibility

There are two aspects of land eligibility that must be fulfilled by afforestation/reforestation projects. In practice, no distinction is made under the CDM between afforestation and reforestation. Therefore, the criterion that all projects must meet is that no land meeting the national definition of forest be present within the project boundaries between 31 December 1989 and the start of the project activity. In other words, land that is eligible for afforestation/ reforestation CDM should have been: (a) non-forest on 31 December 1989; and (b) non-forest at the time of start of project activity.

For the purposes of afforestation/reforestation, non-forest would be any area that does not meet the national definition of forest as communicated by the host party to the CDM Executive Board. The reason for this requirement was the fear that the CDM would create an incentive for land owners to cut down trees in order to make land eligible for credits that would arise if they replanted the land with trees. Proof that land was non-forest can be provided in the form of aerial photographs or satellite imagery from 1989 or before, or official government documentation confirming absence of forests. Where proof of these types does not exist, then multiple independent, officially witnessed statements by local community members can suffice. Evidence of the continued absence of forest since 1989 will also be needed and can take similar forms.

1.3.4 Definitions of Forest

The decision of what constitutes a forest has implications for which lands are available for afforestation/reforestation activities. National presiding authorities in non-Annex I countries, known as Designated National Authorities (DNAs), have been given the role of deciding for their country where to lay the thresholds from the available range determined at COP-9, namely:

- Minimum tree crown cover value between 10 and 30 percent
- Minimum land area value between 0.05 and 1 hectare
- Minimum tree height value between 2 and 5 meters

The following are examples of the implications of forest definitions:

- A high crown cover definition may exclude agroforest projects, but a low definition may make it difficult to include degraded areas with sparse tree cover in the baseline.
- A high value for minimum land area encourages areas with real environmental and biodiversity benefits, but excludes typical community forests and agroforests around dwellings.

- A high tree height value may allow fruit trees as a baseline for reforestation, but could exclude agroforests or other low stature trees in the project scenario.

1.3.5 Added Value to Projects

For projects seeking to have a greater positive socio-economic and environmental impact, it is possible to register with one or more programmes that will give certification if criteria are met. Two notable programmes exist - the CDM Gold Standard (www.cdmgoldstandard.org) and the Climate, Community and Biodiversity (CCB) Standards (www.climatestandards.org).In both cases, the Designated Operational Entity certifies that the enhanced standards are being met, at the same time as validating and verifying the project and the project certified emission reductions. Additional documentation will be required for certification. The standards may also be used at the project design stage to ensure positive socio-economic and environmental impacts. The project would then be able to decide at a later stage whether to follow through with actual certification. The higher level certification will potentially make projects more attractive to investors eliciting a higher value for emission reduction or sequestration credits.

Chapter-2

A Sequential Approach to Develop CDM Afforestation and Reforestation Project

2.1 Overview of the CDM Project Cycle

The ultimate governing body of the CDM is the Conference of the Parties/Meeting of the Parties to the Kyoto Protocol (COP/MOP). The COP/MOP is the annual meeting of the signatories to the Kyoto Protocol and is responsible for managing the CDM Executive Board and for overseeing its work. The Executive Board supervises the CDM process under the authority and guidance of the COP/MOP; it is fully accountable to the COP/MOP. The Board decides on rules for the implementation of the CDM, as well as making the final decisions about acceptance of methodologies, registration of projects and issuance of CERs. The Board is composed of 10 members and 10 alternates. The CDM Executive Board created an A/R Working Group to specifically oversee LULUCF under the CDM. The A/R Working Group provides guidance to LULUCF project developers and, using expert reviewers, makes recommendations on acceptance or rejection of LULUCF methodologies.

Designated Operational Entities, or DOEs, function as auditors for the CDM process. Designated Operational Entities are a domestic or international legal entity, accredited and designated by the Executive Board. They have two key functions: 1) to validate CDM projects prior to project implementation, and 2) to verify and certify emissions reductions after project implementation. An Applicant Entity (AE) is an entity undergoing the approval process to become a Designated Operational Entity. A list of Designated Operational Entities and Applicant Entities can be found on the UNFCCC CDM website (http://cdm.unfccc.int/DOE).

Along with approval and registration by the CDM Executive Board, projects must also be approved by the country in which the project is taking place. The government of each country that is signatory of the Convention will have assigned, or be in the process of assigning, a Designated National

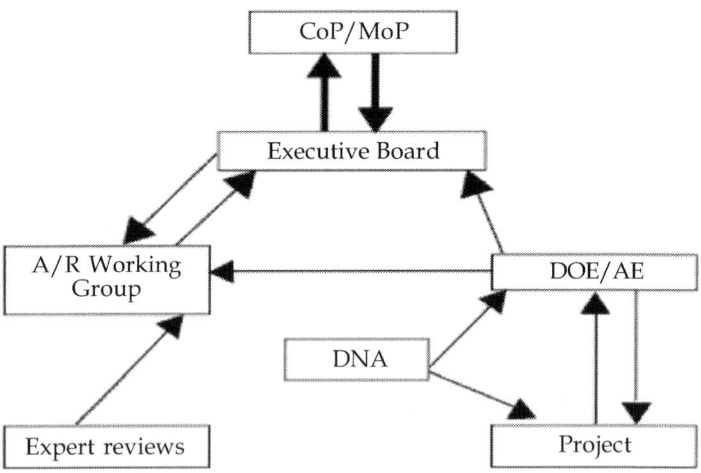

Fig. 3: CDM Cycle Overview

Authority or DNA (the UNFCCC National Focal Point takes on this role). The purpose of the Designated National Authority is to review projects and ensure they are in line with the country's development objectives and national laws. A "host country letter of approval" from the Designated National Authority is required for project registration. Each country may also have its own regulations that must be met to obtain a letter of approval. A list of the Designated National Authorities can be found on the UNFCCC CDM website.

The core of any CDM project is the Project Design Document. The Project Design Document defines the project in terms of activity, length, eligibility, crediting choices, impact and chosen methodology. Creating the Project Design Document is the focus of Section 2.3.

The Project Design Document is prepared by the project participants and submitted to a Designated Operational Entity for validation. Validation is the focus of Section 2.4. Once validated by the Designated Operational Entity (providing there are no objections from the CDM Executive Board), the project is registered and can begin to compile CERs. The methods described in the Project Design Document and implemented by project participants during the project establishment and monitoring are prescribed under the CDM. A project must apply a methodology that has already been approved by the Executive Board. If no suitable methodology exists, the project is obliged to submit its own methodology for approval. This is a long and costly procedure and should be avoided if possible.

Verification of sequestered carbon is also the responsibility of the Designated Operational Entity. Upon verification, the Executive Board can issue tCERs or lCERs. The following diagram illustrates the steps for, and players involved in, project registration and the issuance of CERs.

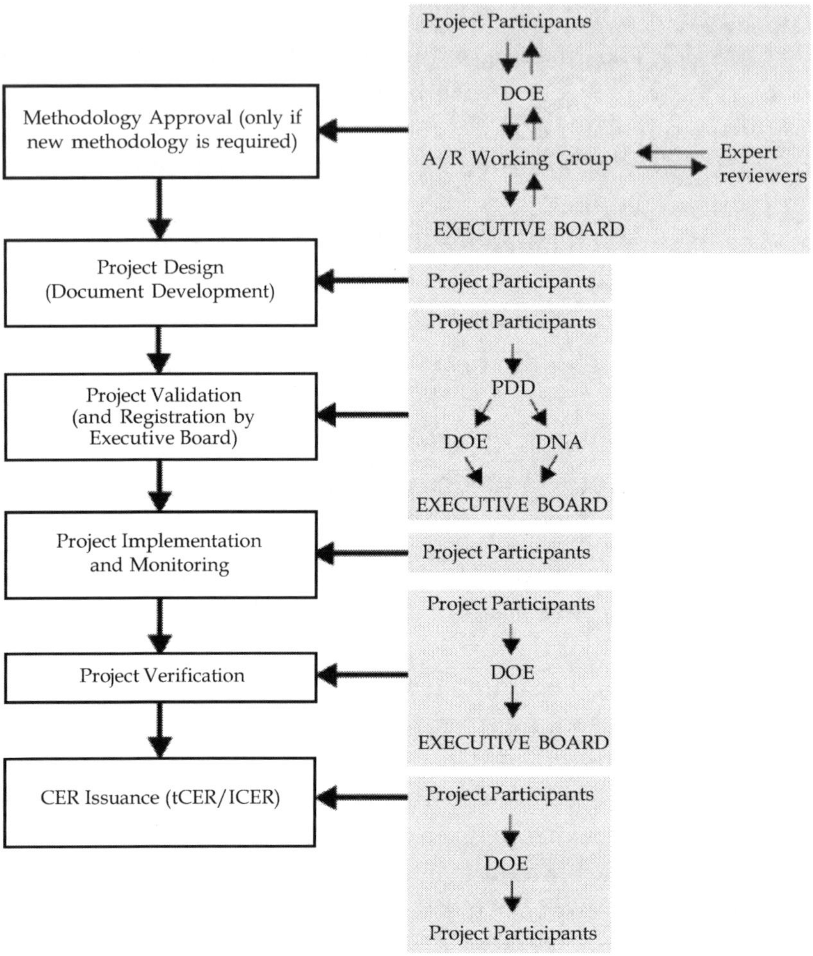

Fig. 4: Detailed CDM Cycle

2.2 Critical Steps for Project Approval

There are eight critical steps in afforestation/reforestation project development and approval is as follows:

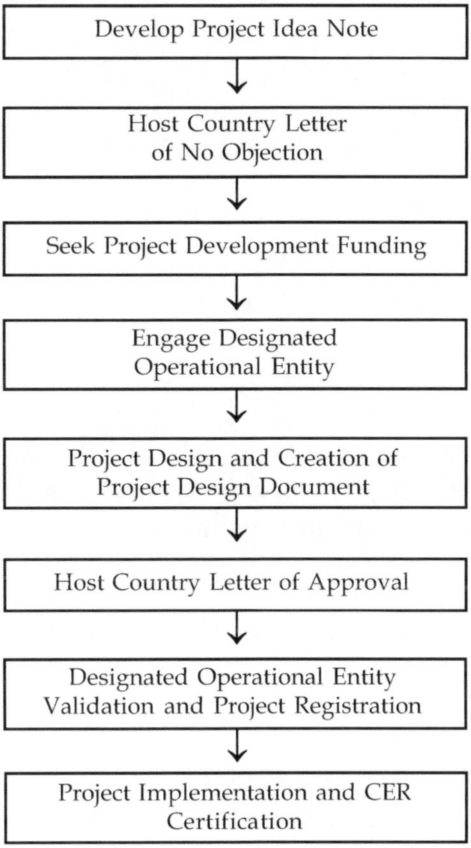

Obtaining a host country letter of no objection at this early stage informs the Designated National informs the Designated National Authority of your plans and prevents future unpleasant surprises.

Entering into an early dialogue with the Designated Operational Entity is advantageous for obtaining advice on choice of methodology and potential future pitfalls.

The letter of approval is critical. Without it, the project cannot be registered.

Fig. 5: Steps of afforestation/reforestation CDM Procedure

2.3 Project Design and Development

2.3.1 Steps in Identification and Preparation of the Project

Project Idea →	Project Development →	Preparation of Project Design Document →	Project Registration
Steps 1-2	Steps 3-9	Steps 10-22	Submit completed Project Design Document to Designated Operational Entity
			Obtain Designated National Authority letter of approval

Fig. 6 : Step wise procedure of CDM cycle procedures

Project Idea

Step 1 : Goals of Project Activity

To help ensure a successful project, the CDM project developer should determine the goals of the project activity.

Determine if the primary goal is:

- Financial profit;
- Providing income for disadvantaged communities;
- Environmental; or
- Greenhouse gas reductions.

The project developer should also determine whether the project location has been fixed prior to the start of project planning or whether it can be chosen to maximise the primary goal. Each of the goals has merit, especially as they each will, in most cases, be intrinsically linked. However, it is important to identify the primary goal as this will strongly drive decision making.

Financial profit

Financial profit has often been a strong driver for CDM projects to date, particularly for investors. LULUCF projects can, theoretically, be profitable. If profit is the motivation, developers should seek sites with minimal risk of leakage, but with relatively easy access and low costs of labour. Profitable projects will typically involve large-scale timber plantations.

Providing income for disadvantaged communities

Sustainable development was envisaged as a central component of all CDM projects and all well-designed projects should positively impact communities – at a minimum providing work and income. Other impacts could be slowing erosion and degradation, protecting critical water supplies, providing a source of wood fuels and providing alternative livelihoods. Projects with the highest impact are likely to be in areas where significant populations exist. Consequently, such projects present an elevated risk for permanence and leakage. Agroforests will usually form a component in community development projects.

Environmental

Environmental impacts can overlap with community impacts - for example, where watersheds are improved and/ or erosion and degradation are halted. However, the projects with perhaps the greatest environmental impact will involve reforesting with native tree species, restoring historic forests and enhancing biodiversity. Such projects are unlikely to be profitable and, beyond the labour for forest establishment, will provide little direct financial benefit to local communities.

Greenhouse gas reductions

Greenhouse gas reduction benefits will often overlap with profit, in that maximising carbon credits is likely to maximize profits. However if profit is the motivation, then the destination of wood products will not be considered and the long-term status of the site beyond the crediting periods will not be an important consideration for the developer. Without these considerations, the sequestered carbon will likely be returned to the atmosphere.

For projects with an explicit community or environmental purpose, it may be advantageous to consider certification under the CDM Gold Standard (www.cdmgoldstandard.com) or the CCB Standards (www.climatestandards.org), as this can increase the attractiveness of the project to investors.

Step 2 : Project Idea Note (PIN) or Project Proposal

Although not a required document, developing a project proposal or Project Idea Note will help solidify the proposed components of the CDM project. Having an established Project Idea Note may also assist project participants in securing investment funding for the project and in discussions with the Designated National Authority and potential regional and local stakeholders.

The Project Idea Note should describe the general goals of the project, what activities will take place to achieve those goals, who potential project participants and stakeholders are, the potential project location, the length of the project, other socio-economic and/or environmental benefits, and, if possible, a very broad first estimate of potential CERs. A good Project Idea Note would comprise approximately five pages. A Project Idea Note will serve as the first form of contact with potential buyers, and will allow project developers the benefit if receiving early feedback on whether the project is of interest to buyers. A critical early step in the preparation of a Project Idea Note is to examine the feasibility of a specific project in the chosen region. This would involve an examination of potential financing and potential sequestration.

Checklist for the Project Idea

1. Determine the primary goal of the project:
   A. Financial;
   B. Developmental;
   C. Environmental; or
   D. Greenhouse gas reductions.
2. Based on this goal, determine the most appropriate afforestation/reforestation activity.
3. Locate a region in which the greatest impact can occur at a cost that is not prohibitive.
4. Prepare Project Idea Note (about five pages).

Project Development

Step 3 : Project Financing Sources

For a CDM project, start-up costs will amount to tens of thousands of dollars. This money is necessary to design the project, gain approval from the host country and achieve validation from a Designated Operational Entity. Therefore, project financing will be required well in advance of the expected pay-outs resulting from the sale of CERs. These start-up funds may be provided by upfront payments for credits, however this form of financing is rare as it is unlikely that an investor will be willing to take on the project risks. Instead, in most cases, funds must be found from grants or loans. Financing should be researched in the following order:

- Countries, companies or organisations that will pay upfront or credits;
- Grants for project development from overseas governments, charitable organisations or charitable arms of companies;
- Loans from international, national or local banks.

Step 4 : Project Management Structure

The next critical step in project development is determining the project management structure. No successful project, particularly in LULUCF, can be solely driven from a distant, industrialised country. It is very important to have motivation and capacity in the project host country. Projects that are designed top-down are doomed to struggle, whereas bottom - up projects will be driven locally at the site where the impacts will be felt and where the required information and data will be derived. On the ground, host country capacity is required in both the understanding of forestry and forestry techniques and in English, which is the sole working language of the CDM Executive Board (although the Project Design Document is available in all six UN official languages).

Step 5 : Local, Regional and National Requirements for Project Development

It is strongly advised to investigate local, regional and national requirements for the anticipated project activities prior to committing substantial resources to project development. These requirements could be specific to the activity, such as regulations governing forest establishment or forest management, as well as CDM-specific regulations.

Step 6 : "Letter of No Objection" from the Designated National Authority

An important project partner will be the UNFCCC National Focal Point in the host country, which is also the Designated National Authority. The Designated National Authority can prevent a project from being registered if it has any objections, therefore it is important to find out all requirements of the Authority for CDM projects. The Project Idea Note can be used to introduce the Designated National Authority to the project and to assist in obtaining the host country letter of no objection at this early stage. This step will also inform the Designated National Authority of project plans and may help prevent future unpleasant surprises.

Step 7 : Appropriate Methodology

Whenever possible, project developers are strongly advised to use to apply an existing approved CDM methodology, as submitting a new methodology to the CDM Executive Board has very large time and financial requirements, and requires a very high level of technical capacity. In addition, it is likely that by the end of 2006 there will be in excess of seven approved afforestation/reforestation methodologies, which should cover most project scenarios. Guidance is therefore given here on how to select from the existing list of approved methodologies to apply to a project. If, however, your project is not eligible to use any of the approved methodologies, it is advised you contact a consultant organisation. The approved methodologies can be downloaded from the UNFCCCCDM website (http:// cdm.unfccc.int/methodologies/ AR methodologies /approved ar .html) and they are presented in Table 1.

Table 1 : Approved Small scale CDM A/R Methodologies

S.No	Specification	Approved CDM A/R Methodology
1.	Simplified baseline and monitoring methodologies for small-scale A/R CDM project activities implemented on grasslands or croplands with limited displacement of pre-project activities – Version 6.0	AR-AMS0001
2.	Simplified baseline and monitoring methodologies for small-scale afforestation and reforestation project activities under the CDM implemented on settlements – Version 2.0	AR-AMS0002
3.	Simplified baseline and monitoring methodology for small scale CDM afforestation and reforestation project activities implemented on wetlands – Version 1.0	AR-AMS0003
4.	Simplified baseline and monitoring methodology for small-scale agroforestry - afforestation and reforestation project activities under the clean development mechanism – Version 2.0	AR-AMS0004
5.	Simplified baseline and monitoring methodology for small-scale afforestation and reforestation project activities under the clean development mechanism implemented on lands having low inherent potential to support living biomass – Version 2.0	AR-AMS0005
6.	Simplified baseline and monitoring methodology for small-scale silvi pastoral - afforestation and reforestation project activities under the clean development mechanism – Version 1.0	AR-AMS0006

7.	Simplified baseline and monitoring methodology for small-scale A/R CDM project activities implemented on grasslands or croplands — Version 1.1	AR-AMS0007

Entering into an early dialogue with the Designated Operational Entity is advantageous, as they can advise on choice of methodology and potential future pitfalls. The Designated Operational Entity can also inform the project developer of exactly what documentation will be required during the certification process. The first step when considering methodologies is to examine the applicability conditions. The applicability conditions must fit your project exactly. If every applicability condition is not satisfied, then that methodology cannot be used.

The project developers should also consider the following advantages and disadvantages of small-scale project activities.The first choice is whether or not to use a small-scale methodology. Electing to be "small scale" limits the project to a sequestration of no more than 8,000 t CO2-e per year. Depending on the species, planting density and climatic conditions, this could be a project of between 200 and 1000 hectares. Currently, there is one approved simplified baseline and monitoring methodology for selected small-scale afforestation and reforestation project activities under the CDM, which can be found at http: // cdm.unfccc.int /methodologies /AR methodologies /AR_SSC_Annex_II.pdf. The limitation in annual sequestration potentially limits the profitability of small-scale projects. There are significant start-up costs, even for small-scale projects, and it is harder to justify these with the resulting small scale of sequestration. However, the methodologies used for small-scale afforestation/ reforestation projects represent some significant simplifications over the requirements for large-scale projects. For example, methodologies for baseline setting, proving additionality and calculating leakage are simplified. It is allowable for an organisation(s) to aggregate or bundle multiple small-scale projects together to maximise efficiency and minimise transaction costs (especially in validation and verification). However, the bundled, small-scale projects cannot be merely a debundled, large-scale project. At a minimum, the boundaries of the small-scale projects should be separated by at least 1km or have different participants (aside from the bundling organisation and the host country).

Potential for leakage

For afforestation/reforestation projects that are not small scale, a significant factor in determining which methodology is most applicable is whether or not there is a significant risk of leakage through activity shifting. Any activity due to the project which will potentially cause greenhouse gas emissions outside the project area must be monitored to assess leakage. Common activities that will need to be monitored include grazing, firewood collection and agriculture. Projects with no activity shifting include projects with no activities currently taking place on the project lands, or projects in which any current activities are not shifted outside of the project boundary. As an applicability condition, the first approved afforestation/ reforestation methodologies (AR-AM0001 and AR-AM0002) require no activities to be shifted outside the project boundary. AR-AM0003 monitors displacement of livestock grazing and agricultural activities, fuelwood collection activities and increased consumption of wood posts for fencing.

Choice of pools

Another important choice in determining which methodology to apply is the selection of carbon pools for measurement. Pool choices include: above-ground biomass, below-ground biomass, dead wood, forest floor (litter) and soil organic carbon.

At COP-9, it was determined that "project participants may choose not to account for one or more carbon pools subject to the provision of transparent and verifiable information that the choice will not increase the expected net anthropogenic greenhouse gas removals by sinks". Therefore, project developers can choose to exclude carbon pools listed in a methodology as long as it can reasonably be shown that the pool will not be smaller in the project than in the baseline.

Trees will form the dominant carbon pool and are relatively simple to measure. Below-ground biomass is typically calculated, rather than measured, and so there is little reason to exclude it. Therefore, all projects should include above and below-ground components of trees. The decision whether to include other pools will be up to each project and the methodology chosen. If any pool will be subject to a loss in the project, then it must be measured. For example, where grasses are replaced by trees, there is a risk in some parts of the world of a loss in soil organic carbon. The potential CERs from the inclusion of a pool need to be compared against the cost of measuring and monitoring that pool with the needed precision. In most projects with duration of between 20 to 60 years, it is unlikely that sufficient carbon will be sequestered in dead wood, forest floor or soil organic carbon to justify the expense of monitoring.

Each methodology has a defined list of selected pools in section I of the methodology. If a developer is intending to include pools in a project that are not included in the CDM methodology, then the project will not be eligible to use that methodology. For example, AR-AM0001, AR-AM0003 and the small-scale afforestation/reforestation methodology include only above- and below-ground carbon pools. Thus, if a project chose to monitor soil organic carbon, then it could not use any of these methodologies. In contrast, as noted above, if it is decided to omit a carbon pool listed in the methodology for a CDM project, this is allowed as long as it can be documented that the pool will not be smaller in the project than in the baseline. AR-AM0002 includes all pools: above-ground, below-ground, forest floor, deadwood and soil organic carbon.

Step 8 : Project Location

If the project location has not been fixed prior to the start of project design, then there is the opportunity to make a project location selection that maximises potential carbon sequestration and minimises start-up costs. To do so, take the following five steps when making the exact project location selection:

1. Assess sequestration potential;
2. Assess eligibility requirements;
3. Assess additionality requirements;
4. Assess environmental and socio-economic impacts; and
5. Assess ability to minimise leakage.

Assess sequestration potential

Physical and human factors will impact the potential sequestration at a project site. Consideration should be given to planting species, topography, slope, elevation, soil fertility, and soil water availability, threat of fire, threat of strong winds, threat of poaching of wood stocks and threat of livestock encroachment.

Assess eligibility requirements

The project location should not be chosen without obtaining prior knowledge of the eligibility of the land. If the area was deforested within the last 20 years, then the entire site might be ineligible. Complex satellite analysis will be required to show the fragments of the land that are, and are not, eligible. The project developer should conduct a simple analysis of imagery from the late 1980s and select deforested areas from that imagery for the choice of project location. Documentation will also be needed to show the land has not been covered by forest at any time since 1990. This can take the form of imagery or other documentation. Eligibility also considers whether the site is below the national thresholds that define a forest. Even if the site does not currently represent your image of a forest, it may still not be eligible because it does not meet the thresholds determined by project host country. The existence of fruit trees or natural regeneration should be warning flags to any project developer that proving eligibility of the site could be a challenge. See Step 14 for further considerations on proving eligibility.

Assess additionality requirements

The additionality of the afforestation/reforestation activity should also be considered when selecting project location. For example, additionality may be a problem if there are national, regional or local government requirements for reforestation in the project area (that have been in place since before 11 November 2001) or if, in the area, timber plantations (such as are being planned for the project) are being established without CDM funding. Without a straightforward additionality argument, a project will not be validated and registered. See Step 13 for further details on proving additionality.

Assess environmental and socio-economic impacts

Any possible negative and positive environmental and/or socio-economic impacts that the project may have on the surrounding area should be considered. Environmental impacts include erosion, impacts on water quality and water supply, impacts from fire and disease risk, and biodiversity impacts. Socio-economic impacts include impacts on local community employment and livelihoods and access to socio-economically valuable resources. It may be possible to alter the location of the project to minimise any possible negative impacts and to maximise positive impacts. At this stage, it is also important to involve the local community and ensure there are no local objections to the project. Local support will greatly aid project validation and if there are objections, it is important to deal with them immediately.

Assess leakage potential

The extent of possible leakage in the proposed project location should be examined. For example, the extent of pre-project activities taking place on the land should be assessed. Additionally, assess the availability of surrounding lands in which potential leakage-prevention measures could take place, and the area and type of land cover on lands where pre-project activities could potentially be displaced.

Checklist for Project Development

1. Establish project finance

Research in the following order:

A. Countries, companies or organisations that will pay upfront for credits;

B. Grants for project development from overseas governments, charitable organisations or charitable arms of companies;

C. Loans from international, national or local banks.

2. Design project management structure

Ensure

A. A division of responsibility for both management- and decision-making;

B. Adequate expertise in forestry and forestry techniques;

C. High capacity in writing and speaking English.

3. Investigate local requirements

A. Designated National Authority requirements for CDM projects; obtain "Letter of No Objection" from Designated National Authority;

B. Local, regional and national laws and regulations for LULUCF.

4. Select approved CDM methodology with the following considerations

A. Determine if project is large- or small-scale. Consider a project composed of bundled small-scale projects if sites are located at least 1km apart.

B. Examine existing approved CDM methodologies and, in particular, applicability conditions to see if they apply to your project. In particular, consider the carbon pools selected and the potential for leakage.

C. Engage Designated Operational Entity and discuss methodology selection.

5. Determine project location taking into consideration

A. Sequestration potential;

B. Land eligibility (that the area was indisputably not forested in 1990);

C. Additionality (that the activity would not have occurred without the potential for carbon credits);

D. Environmental and socio-economic impact;

E. Potential for leakage.

Step 9 : Designated Operational Entity (DOE)

Begin contract negotiations with the Designated Operational Entity, using the Project Idea Note (PIN) to familiarise them with the project. Entering into an early dialogue with the Designated Operational Entity is advantageous, as they can advise on choice of methodologies and the types of documentation that will be required during project validation and registration.

Preparation of Project Design Document

Step 10 : tCERs or lCERs

In response to the permanence issue for LULUCF projects, two types of CERs were created – temporary (tCER) and long-term (lCER) (Section 1.2.3.1). For both types, there is a choice between a single crediting period (to a maximum of 30 years) or a period of 20 years, with the possibility of renewing twice (for a total of 60 years).

Once a CER crediting period is over, the Annex I country must replace this carbon either by purchasing another CER or through the use of Joint Implementation or International Emissions Trading mechanisms. When either type of CER is retired (that is, not sold again), the CDM regulations on that tCER or lCER will cease and the developer is free to harvest the trees if desired. LULUCF tCERs and lCERs cannot be interchanged with CERs issued from energy or industrial sectors and, due to their temporary nature, will be sold at a lower price.

The tCERs

- Expire at end of following commitment period;
- Can be reissued (after verification);
- Must be replaced by buyer when expired with another tCER or an alternative credit;
- Have fees charged for issuance every five years;
- Expire at end of crediting period;
- Provide freedom for project operators, who can retire credits if they choose to harvest or discontinue an area.

The lCERs

- Expire at end of crediting period (20 or 30 years);
- Must be replaced as soon as verification shows carbon stock has decreased, or if there is no verification;
- Are of variable lengths (e.g., an lCER sold after five years might have a duration of 25 years, while one sold after 10 years could last 20 years, etc.);

- Will vary in price based on duration of credit;
- Will have higher prices if long-duration credits, with the benefit of bringing income to project in initial years.

Therefore, lCERs will likely receive a higher price, but commit the carbon for the length of the crediting period. This gives less freedom to the project operator and increases the risks from natural events (lCERs will immediately expire if verification is unsuccessful). Consequently, the default choice for most projects will be tCERs.

Step 11 : Project Duration

Multiple choices exist for project duration, although no project is eligible for crediting for more than 60 years. After initial validation, projects can continue to accumulate CERs for 20 to 30 years without the need for revalidation. If 30 years is selected as the project duration, revalidation is not an option and the project will end at this point. If 20 years is selected, revalidation can occur up to twice to give a total possible project length of 60 years. If the renewable crediting period is selected, then at 20 years (and 40 years), a Designated Operational Entity must determine that the original baseline is still valid. Uncertainties in the climate system are large and it is unlikely that in 60 years, or even 40, that the CDM will still be functioning under current regulations. An argument can therefore be made for the selection of the single, fixed, 30- year period, which removes the cost and potential risks of revalidating after 20 years.

Step 12 : Project Boundary

When the project site, baseline and monitoring methodology have been selected, the next step is to define the project boundary. The project boundary should geographically delineate all sequestrations and emissions that are significant, can be attributed to the project and are under the control of the project participants. Under control typically means that the project operator financially controls the emission or sequestration activity. For example, the project operator will control the growth of trees and use of fertilizer (with the associated emissions) to enhance growth. However, he or she does not control the emissions caused by people physically displaced from the project site by the project activity. The project boundary can include one, or more than one, discrete area(s) of land or parcel. For afforestation/reforestation projects, the boundary is typically simpler than for many energy projects where supply- and delivery-side emissions are complications. In reality, it is often advised to make the perimeter of the areas that will be planted with trees the boundary of afforestation/ reforestation projects. Consideration must also be given to the Designated National Authority's definition of forest in the host country; no one discrete project parcel can be smaller than the minimum area for forest definition.

Project developers should delineate the boundaries of the project ideally using a global positioning system (GPS), or alternatively on a map or georeferenced remote sensing image, prior to submitting the Project Design Document to the Designated Operational Entity for validation. Depending on the methodology used, it may be possible to add in additional areas after the time of validation (e.g., allowed under AR-AM0003).

Step 13 : Additionality Tool

The A/R Working Group, together with the CDM Executive Board, prepared a tool to demonstrate the additionality of projects specifically for the LULUCF sector. The A/R Working Group recommends using the Additionality Tool, although it is not required.The tool can be found at:http://cdm.unfccc.int/EB/Meetings/021/ eb21repan16.pdf. A summary of the tool is also included in Annex E.

At the heart of the tool is the choice to prove additionality through either a financial test or a barriers test, or both. The financial test shows that the project activity is economically less desirable than alternative land uses. The barriers test shows there are barriers to the implementation of the project activity that can only be overcome with CDM finances and that are not present for at least one alternative land use. The financial test is simple to pass for native forest restoration, but could be more difficult for timber plantations and agro forests. The barriers test will apply to most projects, particularly those with a large social impact. It is not advised to select both the financial test and the barriers test, or to select multiple barriers, as proof will be required at validation by the Designated Operational Entity for all tests included in the Project Design Document. The approved methodology chosen by the project will state whether the approved additionality tool or an alternative method must be used to prove additionality is unlikely that any will fail to propose the afforestation/reforestation Additionality Tool. However, if an alternative approach is required, this must be followed. If additionality cannot be proven, the project cannot go ahead under the CDM.

Step 14 : Land Eligibility Tool

There is a mandatory tool for the demonstration of the eligibility of land for afforestation/reforestation projects. The tool must be applied in full in the Project Design Document. It can be found in Section A.4.5 of the Project Design Document, in Annex E and http://cdm.unfccc.int/EB/Meetings/022/eb22_repan16.pdf.

The tool requires proof that the area is not currently forest that it was not forest on 31 December 1989, and that at no intermediate time was it forested and subsequently deforested. This is to be proven either through government documents (the simplest option) or through aerial photographs or satellite imagery complemented by ground reference data. If neither government evidence nor aerial photographs or satellite imagery is available for on or before 31 December 1989, then the option remains of a written testimony produced "following a rural appraisal methodology".

In practice, satellite imagery (e.g., Landsat) is available for most of the world for the late 1980s and can incontrovertibly show lack of forest where the situation is unambiguous. Analysis should be through a supervised classification. It is useful if aerial photographs or other evidence is available to reinforce the classification. Present ground reference data can be used where you have confidence of continuous deforestation beyond the imagery date. Typically, a second image or set of documents is required from a more recent date to show the continuous absence of forest.

Step 15 : Baseline Assessment and Estimation of Carbon Sequestration

A baseline study is required and will form the basis of Annex 3 of the Project Design Document. For the baseline study, it is necessary to follow the selected methodology. The baseline study will define the baseline strata and any emissions or sequestration under the baseline scenario. It is also necessary to estimate the likely sequestration over the lifetime of the project. This is just estimation, however the anticipated growth rate of the trees should be considered, along with all project emissions including leakage.

Step 16 : Leakage Mitigation Plan

Strategies must be developed to prevent leakage from occurring in the proposed project area. If the proposed project area is currently being used by community members, alternative livelihood activities must be created or alternative lands found that minimise the amount of leakage that may take place. For these measures to be successful, they must be both implemented, and continued over the life of the project. This requires strong community support and, ideally, the measures will be positively impacting the livelihoods of the community members. The types of leakage mitigation strategies will be dependant on the pre-project activities, but may include such things as: programmes to increase income or crop yields on non-project lands, or the introduction of alternative livelihoods (e.g., bee keeping, tilapia fish farms, agro forest plantations).

Step 17 : Environmental and Socio-economic Impacts Analysis and Stakeholder Consultations

Sections E, F and G of the Project Design Document have the goal of illustrating analysis of environmental and socioeconomic impacts and demonstrating that stakeholder consultations have occurred at the project site. Each must meet the requirements of the host country. It is good practice to state the legal requirements and how these have been met. Consult with the Designated Operational Entity on the type of documentation that project participants may be required to provide.

Environmental impacts

A formal assessment must be prepared concerning the possible project impacts on the environment. Assessed impacts should include water quality and supply, fire risk, erosion risk, air quality, nutrient/fertilizer run-off risks and endangered species. If there are any negative impacts, mitigation efforts should be carefully designed. The Designated National Authority should be consulted to determine whether the host country requires that a formal Environmental Impact Assessment is conducted.

Socio-economic impacts

This formal assessment should include possible impacts on indigenous peoples, local employment, food production, and access to cultural sites, religious sites, fuel wood and other forest products. It may be recommended to conduct a Participatory Rural Appraisal. The Designated Operational Entity may request official documentation stating that the project will not have any negative-socioeconomic impacts; therefore working with local government officials throughout the project development process will be beneficial.

Stakeholder consultations

Stakeholders must have the opportunity to comment on the Project Design Document. In addition, meetings must be held with stakeholders prior to project registration. Designated National Authority representatives should be invited to these meetings, if possible. The Project Design Document should describe the process by which stakeholders were involved with the project, how comments were invited and compiled, and a summary of the comments must be included. Documentation of stakeholder consultations should be available for the Designated Operational Entity to examine.

Step 18 : Risk and Plan Mitigation Analysis

Project participants bear the consequences of the risks to their activities. If an environmental or meteorological disaster occurs, or if human effects negatively impact stored carbon, then lCERs will be cancelled or fewer tCERs will be available for sale. Part of risk mitigation lies in the positioning of the project. Project location will influence risk of fire or storms, the risk of leakage or other direct negative human impacts. Risk can, however, also be ameliorated in project design. Involving the local community in the project, and providing attractive alternative livelihoods, will reduce human risks, such as poaching, vandalising etc. Natural risks can be lowered by planting patterns, but if these risks are large then it is good practice to retain credits to act as insurance against losses.

Step 19 : Tree-Planting Plan

Although not required as a document for CDM approval, a successful project should also develop a reforestation plan. This plan needs to include the management structure of the planting, the species to be planted, the source of seeds or seedlings to be used in the project (including the possible development of a nursery), site preparation methods, planting methods and a management plan for once the trees are planted. Standard Operating Procedures (SOPs) should be developed for the each aspect of the planting and include quality assurance and quality control measures to ensure project success.

Step 20 : Project Design Document Preparation

The final step of project development is to write the Project Design Document and submit it for validation. The Project Design Document form is included in Annexure. See this Annexure for guidance from the A/R Working Group in writing the Project Design Document, with additional recommendations.

Step 21 : Contract with Designated Operational Entity

Develop a contract for the validation of your project documents by your chosen Designated Operational Entity.

Step 22 : Letter of Approval from Designated National Authority of Host Country

Without a letter of approval from the host country's Designated National Authority, the project cannot be registered.

Checklist for Preparation of Project Design Documents

1. Decide whether to use tCERs or lCERs – tCERs should be the default choice.
2. Determine project duration – 1 x 30 years should be the default choice.
3. Define project boundary – following methods outlined in approved methodology.
4. Apply additionality tool – select barriers test or financial test. If barriers test selected, decide which barrier.
5. Apply land eligibility tool – use satellite imagery, aerial photographs or official documentation to show forest absence on 31 December 1989.

6. Conduct baseline assessment according to selected approved methodology. Determine:
   A. baseline strata (decide and delineate); and
   B. baseline carbon stocks (estimate through measurements).
7. Estimate project sequestration according to selected approved methodology.
8. Develop leakage mitigation plan.
9. Carry out environmental impacts study.
10. Carry out socio-economic impacts study.
11. Hold stakeholder consultations.
12. Analyse risks.
13. Plan to mitigate risks.
14. Create tree planting plan.
15. Write Project Design Document.
16. Agree contract with Designated Operational Entity.
17. Obtain host letter of approval from Designated National Authority.

Step 23 : Project Implementation

Please refer to the Sourcebook for Land Use, Land-Use Change and Forestry for guidance on measurement and monitoring of afforestation/reforestation projects and calculation of carbon benefits. The sourcebook is available at http://www. winrock.org/ecosystems/tools.asp.

2.4 Validation, Registration and Certification

The roles of validation and verification are carried out by Designated Operational Entities under the CDM. Protocols, guidelines and checklists have been created that all major

Designated Operational Entities use in their procedures to ensure their analyses are completed in a credible, independent, non-discriminatory and transparent manner. The CDM and Joint Implementation Validation and Verification Manual can be found at: www.vvmanual.info.

2.4.1. Validation and Registration

The validation process is split into four distinct phases:

Desk Review

On submission of the Project Design Document and accompanying documentation, the first step is a desk review by the Designated Operational Entity. During the desk review, the Designated Operational Entity will specifically examine: project design, the baseline assessment, sequestration calculations, the monitoring plan, and environmental and socio-economic impacts (including the local stakeholder consultation process). In parallel to the desk review, the Designated Operational Entity posts the Project Design Document on the UNFCCC website and invites comments over a 30-day period. Prior to moving to the next phase, the Designated Operational Entity presents the project developer with the first list of unresolved issues.

Interviews and Site Visit Phase

In the second phase, the Designated Operational Entity fields a team to visit the project site. During the site visit, the Designated Operational Entity team interviews project operators, the local community and the host country's Designated National Authority to solicit comments and clarifications. At this stage, the project developer can again review the issues and provide clarifications.

Draft Report Phase

With the release of the draft report, the project developer is issued with the official list of Clarification Requests (CLRs) and the more serious Corrective Action Requests (CARs). This can be the point of greatest delay in the validation process if there is a Corrective Action Request that requires a great deal of work or time.

At the time of the draft report it is also necessary that the Designated National Authority provide the official Letter of Approval to the Designated Operational Entity. The process cannot move forward without this approval.

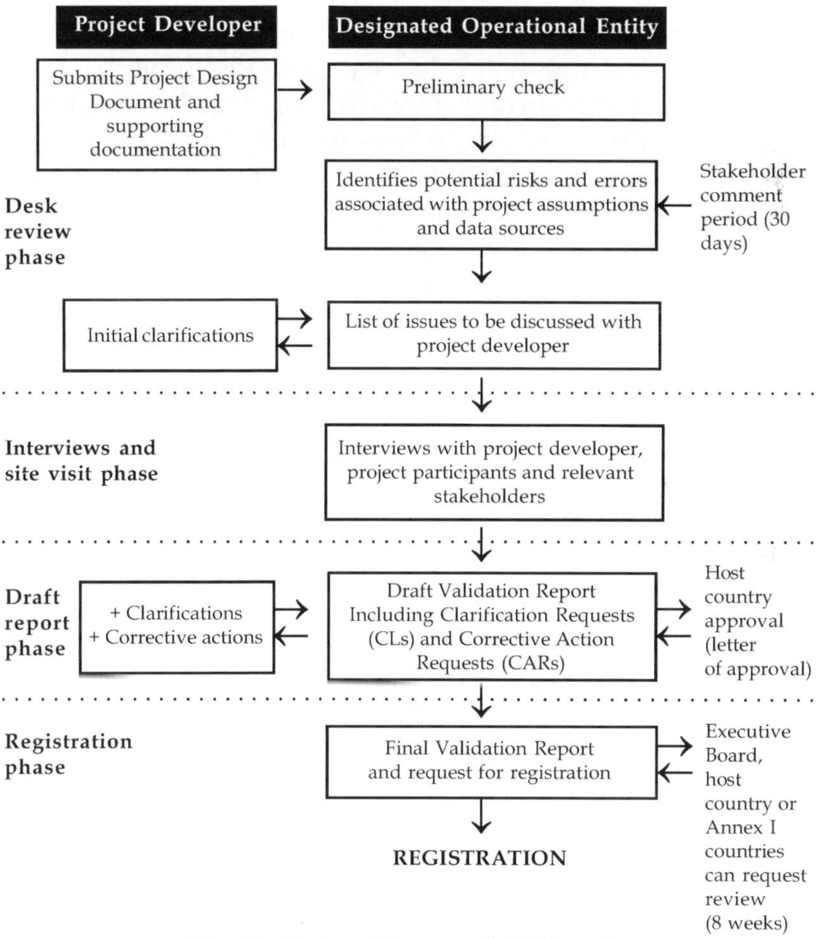

Fig. 7 : Various Phases of CDM cycle

Final Report Phase

The final validation report is presented to the project developer and, if the validation has been successful, the Designated Operational Entity submits the project to the CDM Executive Board for registration. The registration is only deemed final if, after a period of eight weeks (four weeks for small-scale projects), there has been no request for review. Requests for review can come from either three members of the CDM Executive Board or any of the Parties involved in the project.

The validation process typically takes an average of 100 days. It is very important to have a delegated project contact point who can respond quickly to requests from the Designated Operational Entity, so that delays in validation do not arise from the project itself. The desk review and site visit phases typically take from six to eight weeks. Serious delays can arise in receiving the letter of approval from the host country's Designated National Authority (DNA) and from Corrective Action Requests that require significant work and/or time in response.

Commonly encountered errors

Long delays

- Letter of Approval delayed or insufficient;
- Failure to comply with local, regional or national requirements, or missing evidence of compliance;
- Small-scale methodology selected for large-scale projects;
- Non-compliance with applicability conditions.

Short delays

- Lack of logic or consistency in Project Design Document;
- Insufficient information on stakeholder consultation process;
- Lack of justification for deviation from calculation methodology;

- Application of incorrect formulae;
- Project participants not clearly identified;
- Insufficient description of baseline, or lack of supporting evidence for baseline;
- Insufficient explanation of additionality;
- Insufficient proof of land eligibility;
- Major risks to baseline not described;
- Project boundaries not clearly defined;
- Start dates not clearly defined;
- Monitoring procedures not clearly defined;
- Deviations from monitoring methodology not justified.

2.4.2 Verification and Certification

Verification and certification of CERs must be carried out by a different Designated Operational Entity than the one who conducted the validation. After successful verification, the Designated Operational Entity submits a recommendation to the CDM Executive Board for certification and issuance of tCERs or lCERs.

The following list provides an example of some of the facets of the project that may be examined at the time of verification:

- Outstanding issues from validation report;
- Check plantings are as described in Project Design Document;
- Check project boundaries are still in compliance with Project Design Document;
- Check measurement plots and records from plots;
- Examine data uncertainty and quality assurance of measurements'
- Review reporting procedures;

- Personnel capacity - check monitoring personnel have knowledge of methodology;
- Personnel responsibility - check all tasks allocated to sufficiently qualified employees;
- Procedures to record project emissions;
- Leakage - examine leakage calculations and monitoring procedures;
- Data archiving.

Chapter-3

The Global Carbon Market & Financing of Afforestation / Reforestation Projects

3.1 Overview of the Global Carbon Market in Pre-Kyoto Protocol Phase

At the First COP in Berlin in 1995, the UNFCCC launched a pilot phase of projects to build experience and "learning by doing". The pilot phase was termed Activities Implemented Jointly (http://unfccc.int/program/coop/aij/aij_np.html). Under the Activities Implemented Jointly, Annex I Parties could implement projects in other countries that reduced emission of greenhouse gases or enhanced removals of sinks. The number of projects registered under Activities Implemented Jointly has been growing since its launch and as of 2002 (the latest report available) there were 157 projects - 45 percent of which are in developing countries. The total amount of money invested by private sector companies as of 2000 was about $160 million. Because of the expectations that sink projects would be included as a mechanism for achieving targets, several pilot projects were voluntarily implemented involving mostly private sector entities (e.g., electric utility companies, oil companies and environmental non-governmental organisations).Between the beginning of 1996 and the end of 2003, 76 transactions involving carbon sequestration in the LULUCF sector were signed, representing 40 million tCO2-e. Relative to all of the carbon transactions that took place over the same period, sink projects accounted for 21 percent of the total number and 23 percent of the total volume. In volume terms, carbon sequestration projects were the single largest project category, and more than three-quarters of this volume was transacted between 1996 and 1999.

The US Programme on Activities implemented jointly. The US Initiative on Joint Implementation (US IJI), is the largest pilot programme, with more than 25 registered projects. Slightly more than half of the projects are related to the LULUCF sector and most are in developing countries (as of the UNFCCC 2002 report). Many of these LULUCF project activities are non-Kyoto Protocol eligible and, in many cases, involve a combination of forest conservation and changes in forest management. An example of a US IJI project is the Noel Kempff Climate Action Project in Bolivia. In 1996, the Government of Bolivia, the Bolivian conservation organisation Fundación Amigos de la Naturaleza (FAN), American Electric Power and The Nature Conservancy designed a forest-based pilot project to allow for the expansion of Noel Kempff Mercado National Park by adding about 635,000 hectares of land. PacifiCorp and BP Amoco joined the project in 1997. About US$9.5 million has been invested in this project that will generate about 15 million tCO_{2-}e over 30 years.

The advantages of implementing projects under the Activities Implemented Jointly programme is that usually the funds are provided upfront based upon the total amount of carbon credits that potentially will be generated. To obtain the funds upfront, however, a study has to be made demonstrating the feasibility of the project and the likely amount of carbon credits. For example, the US IJI has a detailed description of what needs to go into a proposal on its website (http://www.gcrio.org/usiji/default.html). Private US investors generally require such approval from the US IJI to implement a project. There are several disadvantages of the upfront financing, including: the low carbon "price" (amount invested divided by the estimated carbon credits, most are \$0.3-\$1.4/t CO_2-e or less, although some are as high as \$7.6/t CO_2-e) for the life of project (up to 40 years); uncertainty with respect to companies willing to invest; high transactions costs and low incentives for ensuring permanence, given payments are upfront.

Between 2000 and 2003, the share of sinks projects by total volume transacted sharply declined, in parallel with the US government's withdrawal from the Kyoto Protocol and the limitation of LULUCF to afforestation/reforestation. Although the share declined, 19 sink purchases were concluded in 2002 and another 20 in 2003. One firm, Future Forest, accounted for more than half of the purchases during this two year period. Future Forests' purchases were all for less than 10,000 tCO_2-e and geared towards small individual and corporate clients. Large-scale transactions were considerably less common. However, when measuring the net costs of afforestation, three categories such as planting, management, opportunity costs and benefits must be included. The main reason why afforestation is so widely acknowledged as having large potential throughout the world relates to the rather substantial value of the carbon embodied in forests. Consider a southern upland hardwood forest in the United States, which may typically be harvested at age 50. A stand like this may contain 257 tons CO_2 per hectare in aboveground carbon (Sohngen *et al.*, 2009). If there is no value to carbon sequestration, under current timber prices, such a stand would have a typical return of \$30-\$40 per hectare per year. If, however, carbon prices are \$14 per ton CO_2, then annual returns (inclusive of timber harvests) would be \$75-\$80 per hectare per year, and if they rise to \$28 per ton CO_2, then annual returns increase to \$130-

$140 per hectare per year. The increase in returns to planting forests when the embodied carbon is valued is substantial, for higher carbon prices, it quickly makes forest competitive with some crop and grazing land. Many estimates of the sequestration potential for afforestation have been made over the years. Sedjo (1989) presented the first economic analysis of the potential, finding that forest plantations could sequester up to 10.7 billion tons CO_2 per year for less than $2 per ton CO_2. That study assumed that crop and grazing land was very cheap and could readily be converted to forests. Subsequent analysis suggests that these estimates may be too optimistic – at least with respect to the costs. For example, a global land use model by Sohngen and Mendelsohn (2003, 2007) suggested that 0.7–2.2 billion tons CO_2 can be sequestered globally per year for $8-$30 per ton CO_2. Richards and Stokes (2004), in one of the most thorough reviews of the literature to date, find that 7.0 billion tons CO_2 per year may be sequestered globally, but the costs could be as much as $41 per ton CO_2. All of the estimates discussed in this section account for opportunity costs, and installation and management costs, but not for MMV costs, other transaction costs, or system-wide costs.

Since 2005, much attention has focused on the idea that reductions in deforestation could reduce emissions of carbon dioxide into the atmosphere, and also be a relatively low cost option for mitigation. Of course, deforestation has always been an important contributor to carbon emissions, so it is surprising it took the policy makers so long to get engaged in the issue. Given the scale of deforestation globally, interests among some developing countries to achieve larger reductions in net emissions sooner rather than later, and the interests of environmental non-governmental organizations, avoided deforestation is now widely recognized as a vital ingredient for international climate negotiations. Deforestation causes about 5 billion tons CO_2 emissions per year, or around 17% of total global emissions (IPCC, 2007). From a technical standpoint, avoiding deforestation makes great sense. Standing tropical forests may contain 300-400 tons CO_2 per hectare in biomass (see Kindermann *et al.*, 2008). If these standing forests are converted to agriculture, some wood may make its way into markets, but the vast majority of it will be burned on site when the land is converted. Other wood will decompose over time. Either way, when standing tropical forests are converted to agriculture there is a relatively quick emission of carbon into the atmosphere. Holding that carbon on the landscape in trees can substantially alter net global emissions each year. The value of holding this carbon on the landscape is exceedingly large. If carbon prices are $14 per ton CO_2, the annual rental value of the carbon embodied in a standing tropical forest with 350 tons CO_2 in measureable aboveground carbon is $245 per hectare per year.3 If carbon prices double, to roughly $30 per ton CO_2, then rental values would be $525 per hectare per year. Values this high would compete with agricultural production in some of the world's most productive regions. They are sure to compete with agricultural production in the tropics at the forest-agricultural margin where, by definition, opportunity costs are low. Unlike afforestation, there are no up-front costs associated with planting and managing these forests. One needs to arrange to pay a rental fee to maintain the stock (i.e., to cover the opportunity costs), but these fees do not need to include large-scale outlays to plant and manage timber. The estimates of costs of avoided deforestation presented in this paper thus include only opportunity costs, and losses associated with not harvesting timber. It is widely recognized, however, that there may be some institutional difficulties associated with accomplishing deforestation reductions in developing countries, and thus there may be some other transactions costs that are important. Recent estimates indicate that slowing or stopping this deforestation could have important consequences for the atmosphere. Estimates by Kindermann *et al.* (2008) suggest that for $30 per ton CO_2, around 2.8 billion tons CO_2 emissions per year could be reduced in tropical regions by avoiding deforestation. These estimates in Kindermann *et al.* (2008) are derived from global land use models and they tend to be higher than many other estimates that have so far been done (see Murray *et al.*, 2009). However, even these estimates imply that there is great hope that avoided deforestation can be a low cost option that is meaningfully applied to climate policy. Most of the carbon potential over the 2020-2050 time period results from avoided deforestation in tropical countries, followed by forest management in temperature and boreal regions, and finally by afforestation (Table 2).

Table 2 : Average annual potential net emissions reductions through forestry for the period 2020-2050

	Afforestation	REDD	Management	Total
	Million tons CO per year for the period 2020-2050			
		TEMPERATE		
US	471 (325-2267)[3]	0	291 (268-314)[3]	7
Canada	87[2]	0	148[2]	234
Europe	32[2]	0	132[2]	164
Russia	25[2]	0	414[2]	439
China	104[2]	0	348[2]	451
Japan	34[2]	0	25[2]	59
Oceania	24[2]	0	21[2]	45
Total Temperate	777	0	1378	2155
		TROPICS		
South & Central America	356[2]	1209 (800-1600)[4]	0	1561
SE Asia	288[2]	402 (141-1153)[4]	696[2]	1387
Africa	258[2]	1216 (884-1407)[4]	0	1474
India	168[2]	0	2[2]	170
Total Tropics	1070	2827	698	4595
Total All	1848	2827	2076	6751

Carbon Price assumed to be constant at \$30 per tCO_2. Compilation from various studies. Cost estimates include opportunity costs, and implementation and management costs, but not MMV and other transaction costs.

REDD = reductions in emissions from deforestation and forest degradation; 2 Global Timber Model (Sohngen and Mendelsohn, 2003, 2007); 3 Range from Adams *et al.* (1994), Plantinga *et al.* (1999), Stavins (1999), Sohngen and Mendelsohn (2007), Murray *et al.* (2005), Lubowski *et al.* (2006).4 Kindermann *et al.* (2008).

At \$30 per ton CO_2, 6.8 billion tons CO_2, or about 15% of the total emission of carbon dioxide and CO_2 equivalents currently can be sequestered. What is perhaps most surprising is that the economic estimates presented in Table 1 indicate that the largest share of carbon potential is derived from avoided deforestation (REDD) and forest management. The focus of policy over the past 10-15 years has been on afforestation, and while afforestation is important, it represents the smallest potential share of carbon.

3.2 Kyoto Protocol and the Flexible Mechanisms

The Activities Implemented Jointly programme has now almost completely been replaced by the processes associated with the Kyoto Protocol. In anticipation of Protocol payments, many Joint Implementation and CDM projects were developed before the governing rules had even been determined. These projects benefited through having a long period in which to avoid emissions or to sequester carbon but faced the cost of being the experimental "guinea pigs" for the process. In recent years leading up to Kyoto Protocol ratification, the market for emission reduction credits has been growing rapidly. As an example of the growth, a 38 percent greater volume was exchanged in 2004 than in 2003. As Kyoto ratification occurred in February 2005, an even greater growth might be expected after this date. As an indication of this potential growth, capitalisation of carbon funds grew by 250 percent between

January 2004 and April 2005. Point Carbon estimates traded volumes of 94 million tCO_2-e in 2004 and 799 million tCO_2-e in 2005, which is an 850 percent increase. Sixty percent of the traded volumes were purchased from Europe, two-thirds of which were by private firms and one-third by governments. The Government of The Netherlands alone was responsible for 16 percent of purchased volumes. The demand from private firms seems to be steady while the demand from governments is increasing rapidly.

The project type with the largest proportion of traded volumes has been HFC23 destruction (25 percent of total; all in Asia), followed by capturing nitrous oxide and methane from animal waste (18 percent), and hydroelectric, biomass energy, and landfill projects (each with 11 percent). LULUCF to date has represented zero percent of the traded volumes under the Protocol because, as of March 2006, no LULUCF projects had been fully registered. The market has not been growing as fast as might be expected for two principal reasons. Firstly, the supply response to increased demand is slow as the time necessary for projects to establish and begin to gain credits is slow under the Kyoto Protocol process. Secondly, as governments appear to be the major buyers of the future there is some delay – governments need more time to budget for and purchase than would be the case for the private sector.Outside Europe, demand for project-derived credits is growing with strong indications from both Canada and Japan that substantial amounts of CERs will be required.

The European Union Emissions Trading Scheme (EU-ETS)

With the dominance of European buyers, the European Union Emissions Trading Scheme (EU ETS) has become the dominant player in Kyoto Protocol emissions trading. The EU ETS trades EU allowances (EUAs), which are equivalent to assigned amount units (AAUs).A "linking directive" governs the relationship between the ETS and the Kyoto Protocol. The directive allows Joint Implementation and CDM emission reduction credits to be used (under certain circumstances) against targets under the ETS. Significantly, however, LULUCF projects are currently excluded under the ETS.

3.3 Non-Kyoto Protocol Markets

A proportion of the volume traded every year is outside the Kyoto Protocol system, principally in the voluntary market in the US and in the mandatory market in New South Wales, Australia.In the US, trading of voluntary emissions reduction units can occur on the Chicago Climate Exchange (CCX). LULUCF projects, including forest management and forest conservation, are eligible for this market. As would be expected, project requirements are less than under the Kyoto Protocol flexible mechanisms and this market is likely to see expansion. For example, one Californian electricity company (PG&E) will start offering a scheme whereby customers can volunteer to pay a small premium on their monthly utility bill, which will be used to fund "independent environmental projects aimed at removing CO_2 from the air". In Australia, the New South Wales Greenhouse Gas Abatement Scheme has placed mandatory benchmarks on NSW electricity retailers and other parties.

3.4 Markets Status for Afforestation/Reforestation CDM Activities

3.4.1 Background

Afforestation/reforestation projects are uniquely beneficial as they can be implemented almost anywhere, including Least Developed Countries (LDCs). CDM activities are currently negligible in Africa, particularly if South Africa and northern Africa are excluded. Trees, however, can be planted in the poorest regions and benefit the poorest communities. Terrestrial carbon sequestration was a key topic in the many discussions and negotiations leading up to the Kyoto Protocol, because it had been shown that sinks projects could play an important role at relatively low cost, especially in non-Annex I countries.

Consequently, as already discussed, LULUCF projects formed a significant proportion of the Activities Implemented Jointly portfolio. Many anticipated LULUCF would be just as important under the CDM. At COP-7, it was determined that LULUCF under the CDM should be limited to just afforestation and reforestation. Early start projects began mobilising at this point; in particular with the creation of the A/R Working Group in June 2004. Following the acceptance of the first afforestation/ reforestation approved methodologies in November 2005, it is anticipated that afforestation/ reforestation projects will proliferate.

Fears of permanence and leakage with afforestation/ reforestation LULUCF projects have led to its current exclusion from potentially the biggest CDM market - the EU ETS. It is hoped this decision will be overturned when the positive and secure impacts that LULUCF can make are demonstrated. The scale with which CDM-LULUCF can be used to meet commitments under the Kyoto Protocol is presently limited to 1 percent of the total assigned amount per year of the first commitment period. An additional hindrance to afforestation/ reforestation projects is that they can only attain temporary credits that must eventually be replaced with permanent energy credits. Thus, afforestation/reforestation can only be a temporary solution for any buyer, which in turn leads to lower prices.

3.4.2 Current Market Status for LULUCF Credits

As of the beginning of April 2006, no afforestation/ reforestation projects have been registered and so no lCERs or tCERs have been made available for trading. However, as noted under the Activities Implemented Jointly, LULUCF accounted for 21 percent of trades and 23 percent of traded volume. Outside of the UNFCCC, LULUCF credits have been traded in the New South Wales Greenhouse Gas Abatement Scheme and in the Chicago Climate Exchange.

The futures market is dominated by the Kyoto Protocol. The only notable buyer at the moment is World Bank through its dedicated carbon funds. Nevertheless, there will remain a need for CDM credits for Annex I Parties to meet their commitments. It appears likely that afforestation/ reforestation credits will form a significant supply up to the cap of 1 percent of assigned amounts.

3.5 Financing Afforestation/Reforestation CDM Projects

3.5.1 Costs to CDM Projects

Cost	Estimated Financial requirement
Project development and establishment	US $ 25,000 - 75000
Designated Operational Entity Validation	US $ 10,000 - 15000
CDM registration	US\$0.10/CER for the first 15,000 t CO2-e/year, US\$0.20/CER for any additional credit up to an annual maximum of US\$350,000
Adaptation Fund	2% of CERs issued under project levied for fund to help vulnerable countries adapt to climate change (not for small scale AR projects)
Host Country tax	Some countries will tax CERs using either a standard sales tax or at a CDM-specific rate

3.5.2 Buyers Objectives

The dominant motivation of buyers of CDM credits is to meet their emissions reduction commitments. Currently, it seems that most Annex I countries will have to stretch to reach their emissions reduction goals; consequently pressure is on the demand-side rather than the supply-side. If supply were to exceed demand, then companies, entities and governments could select between International Emissions Trading (governments only), Joint Implementation and the CDM. In this case, CDM is favoured in terms of the auxiliary development benefits and, potentially, cost, but is hindered by at least a perception of enhanced risk of activities in non- Annex I countries. For buyers of credits outside the Kyoto Protocol, the objectives may be to meet non-Kyoto Protocol mandatory emissions reductions, such as in New South Wales or in the northeast US (under the Regional Greenhouse Gas Initiative). Alternatively, under voluntary markets, the motivation may be preparedness for a future mandatory programme or public relations for customers, investors and share holders.

3.5.3 Form of Payment

To date, most projects have followed the commodity model whereby buyers purchase CERs and all risk is carried by the project developer. Very few projects have followed the investment model where payments are upfront. Upfront payments have great advantages for projects, in that project development costs can be covered. However, they are likely to lead to significantly lower prices for CERs as the buyer is then paying for a commodity to be received in the future and is also sharing project risk.

3.5.4 Current Buyers

The BioCarbon Fund

The multilateral funds for carbon projects are overwhelmingly dominated by the World Bank, which facilitates eight carbon funds: the Prototype Carbon Fund (www.prototypecarbonfund. org), the Italian Carbon Fund (ICF; www.carbonfinance.org), the Netherlands Clean Development Facility (www.carbonfinance.org), and the Community Development Carbon Fund (CDCF; www.communitycarbonfund.org),the BioCarbon Fund (BioCF; www. Biocarbonfund .org), the Netherlands European

Carbon Facility (NECF; www.carbonfinance.org), the Spanish Carbon Fund (SCF; www.carbonfinance.org) and the Danish Carbon Fund (DCF; www.carbonfinance.org). The NECF focuses on developing Joint Implementation projects, including possible sinks projects, in Eastern Europe. The SCF will focus on renewable energy and energy efficiency projects. The DCF will not include sinks projects.

All these funds are generally based on the same model. Industrialised countries and companies provide investments (money) that are aggregated in one "pot". These funds, along with other project funding, provide cash flow to host countries and communities to develop carbon projects and produce carbon credits, as well as pre-financing for project identification and preparation activities such as capacity building, outreach and research, leading to the creation of supportive project approval systems in host countries. Funds provided during the project development stage are, for the most part, serving as a loan and are repaid when the project is implemented and carbon credits accrue. The amount of financing will be proportional to the amount of carbon credits the projects will produce, and payment will be made each year as the carbon credits are produced (about \$3-\$6/tCO_2-e). The carbon credits, in return, will go into one "pot", thus generating a mixed portfolio. They are then provided to countries and companies, based upon the amount they invested. The World Bank carbon-financing instruments were created to generate a portfolio of projects that provide benefits to both the host countries and projects as well as to the companies or countries that invest in them. Characteristics of the projects that benefit the host countries include: private capital flows for projects aimed at reducing poverty, investment in cleaner technologies and best practices, ongoing partnerships, and capacity building for communities and intermediaries. For the companies and governments that invest, the benefits include: acquisition of emission reduction credits for compliance, trading, and insurance; cheaper transaction costs; risk mitigation via diversification; knowledge of carbon asset creation; demonstrated social responsibility; and access to additional credits in each deal.

From a practical perspective, there are both advantages and disadvantages to having a project under the World Bank's carbon funds. The advantages include a guaranteed buyer for up to 15 or more years of the project duration at the fixed price initially negotiated; if prices decrease, the developer still receives contract price; and the funds take on much of the risk, address the issue of replacement or retirement of CERs before they expire, and provide technical capacity for designing and verifying the projects. There are very few disadvantages for a project developer to participate in the World Bank funds. A key one may be that if CER prices rise in the future because demand exceeds supply, a project in the World Bank's portfolio is subject to the initially negotiated lower price for the project duration. In addition, all projects entering World Bank-managed carbon funds must satisfy the World Bank operational policies and procedures, including environmental and social safeguard policies.

Buyers outside the BioCarbon Fund

An alternative option for project developers is to obtain financing independently for Kyoto-compliant project development and implementation by developing a business plan like any other venture to raise capital. The CDM Executive Board in February 2005 decided that non- Annex I countries can develop projects without Annex I partners. The CDM Facility of the Asian Development Bank can contribute to this process (www.adb.org/CDMF/default.asp).This CDM facility was established in August 2003 to assist its developing member countries to access development opportunities made possible through the CDM. Its stated goals are to promote projects that contribute to poverty reduction, sustainable development and mitigation of greenhouse gases; lower CDM transaction costs; assist in finding competitive prices for carbon credits arising from projects; and facilitate access to finance by improving project viability. To accomplish these goals, the CDM Facility assists its members to identify CDM opportunities; develop CDM documentation (such as Project Design Documents and new methodologies); move the project through the CDM cycle until it is successfully registered with the CDM Executive Board; and build local capacity. Some funding is available from the CDM Facility to cover upfront transaction costs that the facility only recovers if the project obtains a purchase agreement. These transaction costs include costs for CDM due diligence and regulatory and documentation requirements until the project has been registered and validated. For the first few selected projects, transaction costs will be capped at US$ 100,000.

The advantage of obtaining financing independently is that the project developers can sell tCERs or lCERs at a price the market will bear, but at present the market is uncertain. Disadvantages include: the need for a significant amount of funding upfront to develop and market the "business plan"; the market could be uncertain and risky; and the need for a high degree of capacity to manage, implement and monitor the project. Given the uncertain market, this approach may be more suited to the future when commitments will need to be higher and the market will be more mature and somewhat more predictable.

Options for non-BioCarbon Fund buyers are Annex I governments and individual corporate entities. Unfortunately, the current exclusion of LULUCF from the EU ETS limits the involvement of companies and corporations as afforestation/ reforestation CDM buyers. Consequently, it is likely that governments will be the dominant buyers of credits.

Non-Kyoto Protocol Purchases

As noted earlier, a proportion of the volume of credits traded every year is outside the Kyoto Protocol system, principally in the voluntary US market and the mandatory market in New South Wales. In the US, the voluntary nature of the market leads to low prices for traded units, typically between \$1-\$2 tCO_2-e. This market is likely to see expansion. In Australia, the New South Wales Greenhouse Gas Abatement Scheme has placed mandatory benchmarks on NSW electricity retailers and other parties. Under this mandatory scheme, prices have averaged US\$8.1 tCO_2-e.

3.5.5 Funding for Project Development

Sources of funding for project development include:

- Grants and subsidies;
- Upfront payments for credits;
- Soft loans and loan guarantees;
- Commercial lending;
- Equity investment into companies; and
- Investment into other income-generating activities.

3.6 Risks and Uncertainties

3.6.1 Risks to Project Developer

As the project is typically paid on delivery of the temporary CERs, the dominant portion of the risk rests with the project developer (the seller). Risks to the seller refer to any event(s) that negatively effect the expected greenhouse gas (and consequently financial) benefits to the project. These risks include:

- *Natural risks*: fire, disease, lower than predicted growth rates, drought, floods, damaging winds;
- *Anthropogenic factors*: encroachment, poaching, fire, vandalism;
- *Political risks*: policy changes, unstable governments;
- *Economic risks*: exchange rates, interest rates, lower than expected tCER/ lCER prices, changes in opportunity cost of land. Risks are particularly acute where lCERs have been selected as the form of credit – lCERs have an initial duration equal to the length of the crediting period but

expire immediately if the stored carbon has diminished at the next verification.

3.6.2 Risks to CER Purchaser

As stated above, under the CDM system risk is concentrated with the seller. However, this is not the case where there has been an upfront payment for CERs or where a particular supply of credits is relied upon by the buyer to fulfill an assigned amount commitment afforestation and reforestation under the CDM.

3.6.3 Risk Mitigation Mechanisms

Buyers can mitigate their risk by only paying upfront for projects in which they have high confidence of successful delivery. Confidence should be attained through examining the risk mitigation activities and policies of the seller. As the greatest risk lies with the seller, the seller retains the greatest opportunity and responsibility for risk mitigation. Beyond deciding optimal project location and planting design, policies can be implemented to further mitigate risks to the project, examples include:

- "Good practice management systems" to control the occurrence of, and the response to, damaging events;
- "Self-insurance reserves" where a portion of tCERs or lCERs is kept as reserves against a future shortfall. If damage does not occur, then the reserve can be sold at the end of the crediting period.
- Involvement of stakeholders. Retaining the involvement of stakeholders beyond the initial project design period retains good will and reduces risks of poaching or malicious damage. Stakeholders can be further incentivized through the transfer of technologies and the implementation of activities that will directly benefit the community.

Chapter-4

India's Response to the Carbon Market Policy and Challenges

As a developing country, India does not have any emission reduction target, but it is able to sell CERs pursuant to the CDM, to large emitters covered by the EU ETS, countries that have emission reduction targets under the Kyoto Protocol, or any other entity that wishes to purchase such CERs for compliance purposes. It can also supply ERs and VERs for the growing voluntary markets.

4.1 Status and Trends

India's participation in the carbon markets has contributed to the recognition that it is a useful tool in attracting climate friendly investments. India was an early player in the market, and it used the hosting of the Eighth Conference of Parties to the UNFCCC in Delhi in October 2002 to sensitize the business community about the opportunity provided by carbon finance and the modalities of the emerging CDM. In 2004, the growth in the Indian carbon market was fostered by a healthy number of indigenous management and technical consultants, which began to offer services to potential sellers of emission reductions, and the response from primarily the private sector to capacity building initiatives concerning the nascent market. In its capacity as the Designated National Authority (DNA) for the CDM, the Ministry of Environment and Forests (MOEF) also had the foresight to develop simple and transparent rules, whereby project developers can obtain a Letter of Approval (LOA) theoretically within sixty days, which is a key step required for project registration. By the end of 2004, India was the market leader in the forward sale of emission reductions, with 50 % of the supply market. Early successes included the registration of two projects which consisted of the thermal oxidation of HFC-23 generated as a buy-product during the manufacturing of the refrigerant HCFC-22, but also a number of small scale co-generation projects using bagasse, rice husk and mustard crop residues as a source of biomass, and small scale hydropower projects.

As the Kyoto Protocol came into force and the EU ETS was enacted, China entered the carbon market in full force in 2005. At the same time, many buyers reported that it was becoming difficult to close deals in India in 2005, as carbon prices, in particular for EUAs sold pursuant to the EU ETS, began to rise. Even in the absence of price transparency for CERs and other asset classes, many sellers in particular from India, showed a great risk appetite as they expected prices to also continue to rise, and attempted to add value to their CERs through project registration. As a result, India dropped to third place in the global supply of project-based emission reductions in 2005 (at 3%), behind China (73%) and Brazil (11%).

Following the volatility in prices in 2006, many sellers in the carbon market became aware of the need to adopt risk hedging strategies given the highly volatile nature of the CDM and other nascent carbon markets. This was particularly true in India, where many sellers preferred to implement projects "unilaterally," i.e., without cooperation with a buyer, because they preferred to register the project and later sell issued CERs, rather than sell VERs or forward sell their CERs, whose prices are discounted due to project, delivery and transfer risks. The Integrated Energy Policy issued by the Indian Planning Commission in August 2006 for instance recommends that India consider selling emission reductions at a later date when such selling is more attractive, presumably referring to better prices. While it is difficult to assess the extent to which Indians hold on to their CERs to maximize price in the absence of a full market study, there is some anecdotal evidence that this behavior is not as prevalent now as it was before the EUA price fluctuations experienced 2006.In 2007, India's market share, measured in value of signed Emission Reduction Purchase Agreements for either spot or forward sales, was at 6% in 2006, second only to China which supplied 73%.

Other indicators reveal that India ranks:

- first by number of projects registered by the CDM EB at 345 followed by China's 221. Of these 61 % were small scale projects (212),
- second by number of projects in the UNEP/RISOE pipeline when considering the total number of projects at validation, requesting registration and registered (1252 projects for China vs. 966 for India) as of June 2008
- second by volume of issued CERs at 42.9 Mt CO2e (coming mainly from two HFC23 projects), after China's 44.6 Mt but before South Korea's 27.2 Mt. and 21.5 Mt for Brazil as of June 2008
- second in the UNEP/ RISOE CDM pipeline in the number of expected CERs by 2012 at 353 MtCO2e (or 15.7%) when including HFC23 assets (compared to China at 1187 MtCO2e or 52.7% and Brazil at 155 Mt or 6.9%) as of September 2007
- third by share of signed emission reduction purchase agreements since market inception, when HFC23 assets

are excluded from the analysis, as follows: China (40%), Brazil (15%) and India (8%) as of September 2007

- India also has the largest number of projects rejected at the registration stage (29) and withdrawn

4.2 Response Analysis

What emerges from the above analysis of trends is that as an early mover in the supply market, India is performing well compared to China in the expected volume of CERs to be delivered by 2012. While China's supply to the CDM market should be 4 times that of India when taking into account current greenhouse gas emissions, China will deliver 3.5 times as many CERs as India by 2012.However, it is certain that beyond 2012, China will outperform India in the carbon market, given that (i) it has already surpassed the Indian number of projects taking into account the total number of projects under validation, requesting registration and registered and (ii) the average project size in China is 2.72 times that in India's. Consequently, it is expected that China will have a CDM supply market of 4.75 times that of India beyond 2012 when considering projects registered until 2007 and much larger once the projects currently in the pipeline are registered. What is more troublesome is that China is significantly outperforming India in market access. China is the preferred destination of buyers of emission reductions, and China sold five times the emission reductions than India since market inception. This can be partly explained by the fact that Chinese project developers must identify the sellers when requesting a Letter of Approval from the DNA, whereas a good number of Indian project developers prefer to seek to maximize price by first registering the project and selling once the emission reductions are certified, which creates more value added albeit at higher risks.The Chinese DNA also selectively promotes specific sectors that have been assigned priority for the CDM, many of which target the meeting of national energy efficiency and generation targets. However, the troublesome fact is that the vast majority of Indian projects are small in scale (60% of projects registered so far), and in the absence of aggregation, these are of less interest to carbon buyers given the amount of due diligence and transaction costs required to purchase significant volumes, and this reduces the negotiating power of individual project developers and increases project risks.

It is also conceivable that the sale of issued CERs will compete at some point prior to 2012 with the sale of large volumes of assigned amount units (AAUs) which are a form of emissions allowance pursuant to International Emissions Trading (IET) according to article 17 of the Kyoto Protocol that are available in ample quantities particularly from Russia and the Ukraine to meet any gap that industrialized countries may have in meeting their emission reduction targets.

The Indian carbon market is largely driven by small and medium enterprises (SMEs), which are not surprising, as India has nearly three million SMEs which constitute more than 80 percent of total number of industrial enterprises in the country. According to recent estimates by the Indian Institute of Foreign Trade, approximately 60 percent of the country's GDP comes directly or indirectly from SMEs. In the absence of price transparency, it is not clear that project developers from SMEs have the necessary information about market fundamentals to develop sophisticated risk-hedging strategies in a highly volatile market. Although there are a number of brokers and consultants available in the Indian carbon market, price projections vary widely. Hence small projects and SMEs are largely disadvantaged in the current carbon market. The public sector in India has also been relatively absent from the carbon market. Of the 333 projects registered at the CDM EB from India, only 16 originated from public sector units (PSUs). Even among these, 10 use small scale methodologies. This is particularly noteworthy since public spending still dominates key candidate sectors for CDM.

4.3 Carbon Market Barriers in India: Policy and Challenges

The GOI is facing some international pressure to adopt an emission reduction target for the second commitment period of the Kyoto Protocol. India maintains that it will not adopt a target, as this would negatively impede its economic growth and poverty reduction objectives. In that context, the CDM remains one of the major financial tools at India's disposal to participate in global efforts to mitigate greenhouse gases. The UNFCCC estimated that that should the industrialized nations adopt an aggressive emission reduction target of 50 % or more by mid-century, and should they meet half of their emission reduction commitments through the purchase of project-based emission reductions from developing countries such as India, the CDM market could grow to a level of $100 billion sales annually (a growth of 20 times compared to 2006). That means that CDM could be on par with ODA as a source of foreign capital flowing to developing countries. That is of course an upper boundary estimate of the potential market size. The relative demand for emission reductions from industrialized countries will depend on the nature of the second commitment period of the Kyoto Protocol (post-2012), and in the absence of such an agreement, the demand from regional and voluntary markets, as well as policies in industrialized countries. In that context, it will be important to note the discussions on supplementary, where countries that are net buyers may wish to limit the quantity of offsets available from developing countries. Typically, proponents of strong limits on the import of carbon offsets from developing countries cite the need for domestic action to address climate change and competitiveness issues to support their position. There is unfortunately no market data available specific to India's participation in the carbon market. From global data, it is estimated that as of the end of 2006, India has entered into emission reductions transactions representing more than 111.6 $MtCO_2e$ (of which 70 $MtCO_2e$ came from HFC-23 projects), with an approximate value of $800 million, leveraging climate friendly investments of $2.25 billion.

4.3.1 Uncertainty in the Second Commitment Period of the Kyoto Protocol

It is well documented that long term commitments by industrialized countries are needed to ensure the long term viability of the carbon markets, including the CDM, as these establish a demand and value for emission reductions. In the absence of such commitments, demand for emission reductions will be driven by regional markets such as the EU-ETS, including any post-2012 phase, and other regional regimes which allows the introduction of offsets.

In January 2008 the EU Commission adopted a proposal regarding the design of the EU ETS post-2012. For projects started /registered after 2012, issued CERs can only be introduced from least developed countries. If an international agreement is reached regarding the second commitment period of the Kyoto Protocol (i.e., after 2012), 50% of the additional commitment can be achieved through the CDM from participating countries. In essence this means that the largest demand for CERs will dry up from large developed countries like India if there is no agreement on a second commitment period of the Kyoto Protocol.

In India, the continued uncertainty of any agreement regarding the second commitment period means that there will be an increased emphasis on projects with short lead times, such as demand side energy efficiency projects, and projects that are already under sound financial footing, i.e., where the financial closure does not strictly depend on the forward sale of emission reductions. This means that carbon finance has limited influence in investment decisions for large scale infrastructure projects with long gestation periods that have the potential to deliver a large quantity of emission reductions until the uncertainty is significantly reduced.

4.3.2 Lack of Concerted Strategy

So far, the GOI has considered the CDM and by extension carbon finance to be strictly market based mechanisms, and has decided therefore not to interfere through any targeted programs or funds to increase or promote any specific programs. It has however fostered the growth of the market in India through capacity building initiatives, and the setting of clear and transparent guidelines for project approval. However, it is becoming increasingly clear that China is dominating this market, and has partnered with many international organizations to address any gaps and advance the use of carbon finance to meet national objectives. China is also about to launch its CDM Fund which will further develop its domestic market. The GoI should respond through the development and implementation of a national strategy on carbon finance to further advance the use of this market mechanism.

4.3.3 Lack of Methodologies

Several asset classes have limited potential to deliver emission reductions as follows: (i) the parties to the Kyoto Protocol have informally agreed to refrain from introducing nuclear power projects under the CDM, and no regional regime has ever recognized carbon assets from nuclear power (ii) land use, land-use change and forestry assets in the CDM are limited to afforestation and reforestation activities and (iii) the EU ETS does not allow the introduction of any assets from land use, land-use change and forestry, including those from afforestation and deforestation, and has limited the introduction of carbon assets from hydropower projects to those that meet guidelines issued by the World Commission on Dams.

Most regional regimes require the use of approved methodologies to establish baselines and monitoring plans for carbon offset projects, and the CDM is certainly the most advanced regulatory regime in this regard. For illustrative purposes, Table- 3 provides a preliminary analysis of the status of approved methodologies under the CDM for the main actions recommended Integrated Energy Policy Report. For addition of capacity to the grid for example, sub-critical coal is expected to remain the least-cost option for the foreseeable future for most parts of the country, and thus other options such as renewable energy, ultra-supercritical and efficient gas should remain eligible for carbon finance as long as their costs are not competitive with other generation options in the India market. There are a number of methodologies that have been adopted in the energy sector, although their ability to assist in the development of the sector remains limited. Of note are the following methodologies: capacity additions to the grid from renewable energy, captive power plants from biomass or natural gas, new grid connected fossil fuel fired power plants using a less greenhouse gas intensive technology7, and fuel switching to less greenhouse gas intensive fuels. However, there is a notable absence of either methodologies or application of methodologies compared to the potential for carbon finance in particular from India. This is true for demand-side management measures (which has the highest potential for generating emission reductions in the short term), improved efficiency of coal and hydropower plants, the introduction of best available technology in energy intensive sectors and higher freight share of railways. In some cases where project activities exist, modifications to methodologies through resubmissions to the CDM EB would be required if carbon finance is to be scaled up and contribute to large scale investments in lower carbon technologies, taking into account local conditions.

At face value, carbon finance and the CDM in particular should contribute to India's efforts to provide lifeline energy to all households and electrify the 400 million poor by 2012, and to assist the development of the large hydro potential from the mid-Himalayan region. In the case of rural electrification, the CDM EB had been reluctant to approve a methodology that would recognize the substitution of non-renewable biomass (i.e., fuel wood), which is the fuel of choice for the world's poor, although two such methodologies will be considered at the next Conference of Parties. As the inclusion of hydropower in the CDM does not have full consensus among all stakeholders, the outcome of any request for registration from such projects is not certain.

Table 3: Preliminary Assessment of Status of Approved Baseline and Monitoring Methodologies According to Main Actions Recommended in the Integrated Energy Policy

Relevant Recommendation	Current Situation with Regard to CDM Methodology	Way Forward
Relentlessly pursue energy efficiency	Methodologies exist for some activities (ACM 12, AM 20, AM 44, AM 46) Small scale Methodologies also available (AMS IID, AMS II E)	Move away from project by project approach. Identify positive list of technology applications. Develop tailored applications for several sectors; particularly the building sector; industrial and household
Develop fully the nuclear and hydro option	Parties to the Kyoto protocol have agreed to refrain from introducing nuclear power project in the CDM; Methodologies for hydro already available as part of renewable (ACM 2)activities	Explore feasibility of expanding the use of CDM to large hydro and forced hydro
Undertake pilot projects in biomass plantations and biofuels	Approved methodologies for grid connected biomass plantation based electricity (AM 42); other biofuel methodologies awaiting CDM EB approval	Approve new/existing methodologies with appropriate caveats and practical approach for assessing upstream emissions which does not require full life cycle analysis

Undertake solar technology solar thermal economically attractive	Solar Power usually used only on small scale (AMS IC and ID) and as part of ACM 2	Demonstrate application of methodology for solar thermal on a large scale
Assess off-shore wind power potential	Already covered under renewables (ACM 2)	Demonstrate appropriate incentive schemes/policies and pilot program of activities
Improve coal power plant efficiency	Methodology for efficient new technology plants recently approved (ACM 13)	Develop new methodology for R&M of power Plants
Produce biodiesel in a decentralized manner and substitute all agriculture use of HDSO/LSHS/Fuel oil with biodiesel	Biofuels are not yet approved by CDM EB; except from waste cooking oil (AM 47)	Encourage development of Program of Activities around biodiesel and straight vegetable oil for agriculture sector
Improve Railways' freight services for long distance goods traffic	No modal shift methodologies for rail to road approved	Develop a CDM PoA around increase of Indian Railway's share of Freight traffic
Promote urban mass transport to reduce demand for personal motorized vehicles	BRTS methodology approved (AM 31)	Develop CDM projects with Rail MRTS
Improve fuel efficiency of motorized vehicles by a factor of two through vehicle design	No methodology approved	While this is being done in collaboration with manufacturers' explore CDM potential of improvement of road infrastructure for inter-city traffic

Hence, the lack of approved baseline and monitoring methodologies or methodologies which are applicable to domestic conditions remain a formidable barrier to the growth of the carbon market for some sectors where the CDM could potentially make a significant contribution. If the CDM is to realize its full potential, it is clear that methodologies have to be applicable to entire sectors, rather than their current limited application on a project by- project basis. Already project developers have demonstrated the use of bundling, which allows the aggregation of a number of small activities under a single project, provided the individual activities are known at project registration. The recently adopted rules on programs of activities (POAs), which allows for a verification of individual activities ex-post from registration, should further expand the use of the CDM. However, more standardization is required to facilitate the broadening of methodologies and specific components to the sector level.

4.3.4 Lack of Incentives to Reduce Emissions in the Public Sector

The carbon market has really captured the imagination of Indian entrepreneurs, and there has been a significant amount of awareness-raising regarding the carbon market. However, in most organizations including PSUs, the task of identifying the opportunities provided by the carbon market has been assigned to an individual, who often has other responsibilities, rather than a dedicated CDM cell. There are notable exceptions. In June 2007, the Ministry of Urban Development (MOUD) established a High Power CDM Committee to disseminate technical and financial information regarding carbon finance, and promote the use of the CDM in the urban sector. A capacity building program lead by the MOEF has identified a number of intermediaries at the state level. However, there is a lack of incentives for PSUs to undertake CDM projects, in particular because it is not always clear whether CDM revenues will accrue to the project or entity that successfully implemented the project. Other factors that contribute to the lack of involvement of the PSUs in the market include: procedural constraints in engaging with foreign agencies, lack of data management systems and concerns regarding disclosure of data.

4.3.5 Lack of Aggregation for SMEs

For many buyers of emission reductions, India is not an attractive destination to purchase emission reductions, as the majority of projects are small scale and do not meet their minimum size requirements. Although buyers can aggregate a number of small projects into larger ones, they prefer that this function be managed by the sellers in order to reduce the amount of due diligence required and to reduce transaction costs. In some sectors, notably for energy efficiency measures in the brick construction and steel forging sectors, natural intermediaries emerged, such as technology providers or industry associations. Such intermediaries were able to aggregate a number of small projects into larger ones, which improved market access and reduced transaction costs. In another recent example, the Bureau of Energy Efficiency (BEE) is developing a program of activities under the CDM for the substitution of incandescent lights with compact fluorescent lamps (CFLs). However, despite a number of capacity building efforts in the country regarding aggregation and intermediation, the market remains fragmented.

4.3.6 Relative Absence of Financial Sector

A supportive investment climate for CDM projects such as renewable energy projects requires a well designed regulatory and policy framework that helps to remove the barriers for implementation of renewable energy projects and enables efficient utilization of renewable resources by providing positive incentives for efficient renewable options.

One of the concerns expressed by potential investors has been that in recent years the regulatory framework for renewable energy in India has become uncertain, having an adverse impact on the investment climate. Similarly, there has been a reluctance of commercial banks in India to lend for energy efficiency measures, which may improve the bottom-line, but does not necessarily directly contribute working capital that builds fresh production capacity. Within this investment climate, very few Indian banks provide lending using a project finance model, which would lend itself well to take into account an additional revenue stream such as carbon finance. More often than not, Indian banks would heavily discount the carbon revenue stream, in part due to lack of knowledge or uncertainties regarding the carbon market, and would not consider Emission Reduction Purchase Agreements as part of collateral or guarantees to finance a project with climate-friendly technologies. Consequently, there are very few indigenous examples to date of the use of financial engineering to improve lending terms, reduce project risks or monetize or securitize revenue flows from CDM projects. The vast majority of CDM projects are either financed on the balance sheet or financed without taking into account potential carbon finance revenues, which are seen as an upside.

4.3.7 Lack of Price Transparency

Unfortunately, there is no real-time price discovery for CERs. Apart from the European Climate Exchange that accounts for 80 % of the trades in EUAs so far, there is no international platform with sufficient liquidity where prices of CERs can be benchmarked. Even EUA prices under the European Climate Exchange are not a good indicator of CERs prices for Indian projects, as these would depend on issues such as default risk, financial strength of sellers, as well as registration and project related risks.

While the large multinational companies from India will have access to CER pricing information, the SMEs and PSUs, which rely on bilateral and over-the-counter transactions, are at a disadvantage because of the lack of sufficient price related information (i.e., factors that determine price), poor negotiating capabilities and poor access to international markets. Given the volatile nature of the carbon market, there is a need for more transparency in pricing of CERs and an efficient system for the dissemination of information regarding market fundamentals that could better inform potential sellers regarding risk hedging strategies. Price discovery mechanisms that allow project developers to seek bids from numerous buyers through either an auction or a platform using standard contracts are beginning to emerge in part to fulfill the need for greater price transparency.

In September 2007, the European Carbon Exchange launched a futures and options contract for CER as an alternative to over-the-counter CER contracts. The Brazilian Mercantile and Futures Exchange has been trying to establish a carbon trading platform in Brazil and recently auctioned CERs from a public sector project (see 4.3.7.1). The Asian Carbon Exchange hosted in Singapore has been facilitating electronic auctions of PDDs and issued CERs followed by out of exchange settlement, along the lines of a brokerage model, since 2005. Eurex and the European Energy Exchange(EEE) have also declared their intentions to launch CER futures contracts. The Japan Bank for International Cooperation (JBIC) is establishing a trading platform and national registry with the participation of number of trust banks to clear and settle trades involving Japanese companies. These platforms are expected to supplement over-the-counter CER contracts and allow users to lock-in prices delivered at set dates in the future, which will contribute to a much more transparent and robust CER market.

Brazil has been a pioneer in the carbon market and considers project-based greenhouse gas emissions trading as an important tool to reach its development objectives. While substantial progress has been made, Brazil has yet to reach its full potential in the carbon market, due to the lack of key infrastructure that would promote market access, and barriers faced in particular by the public sector units (PSUs) and larger industrial companies. The key barriers include the absence of clear regulatory and market mechanisms that would allow the selling of CERs other than through the bilateral and over-the-counter transactions, and the lack of financial instruments to enhance the value of CERs in a volatile market. Recognizing these constraints, the Brazilian Mercantile and Futures Exchange (BM&F) and the Brazilian Ministry of Development, Industry and Foreign (MDIF) Trade entered into a Memorandum of Understanding (MOU) in 2004 to develop and implement the Brazilian Emission Reduction Market (BERM), with the purpose to develop a trading platform for the futures and spot transactions for CERs. In 2006, the Government of Brazil signed a grant agreement with the Japan Policy and Human Resources Development (PHRD) fund managed by the World Bank, to support BM&F's ongoing efforts and strengthen the financial infrastructure and institutions of the Brazilian carbon market. The specific activities covered by the grant include:

- An outreach program with selected key industry groups that have not yet benefited from the carbon market
- The provision of technical assistance to such industries to prepare carbon finance activities in these industry groups
- The development of a system for the marketing of the CERs and various related financial instruments in a manner that is consistent with Brazilian regulations and procedures for public entities
- An outreach and technical assistance effort to engage the financial sector in Brazil to participate in the carbon market
- The promotion of a trading platform for the sale of certified emission reductions

Through these efforts, BM&F successfully launched on September 26, 2007 a public auction for the sale of 800,000 tCO_2e of issued CERs from a single landfill project of the Municipal Government of Sao Paolo, which settled at a price of € 16.20 /tCO_2e.

However, these emerging trading platforms and auctions are expected to have a limited appeal to Indian project developers, in particular for SMEs and PSUs, due to a lack of presence and credibility in the Indian market and lack of regulatory certainty regarding the public trade of CERs. As well, the trades under these emerging auctions and platforms are small in volume, and they are not true indicators of price for Indian CERs. Several domestic entities, most notably the National Commodities and Derivatives Exchange (NCDEX) and the Multi Commodity Exchange of India (MCX), have proposed the establishment of domestic carbon trading platforms. However, the establishment of a carbon trading platform in India faced a number of regulatory barriers, since emission reductions are neither defined as commodities or services, and there is a limited regulatory regime to allow the forward trading of intangible commodities, i.e., those commodities that cannot be physically delivered. The Forward Contract (Regulation) Act, 1952 (FCRA) specifically requires the physical delivery of the regulated good, and it is not clear that CERs could meet the current legal definition of goods without a regulatory amendment. In early 2008, a notification has been issued by the government, allowing trading in carbon credits on the commodities exchange and would thus be regulated by the FMC.

4.3.8 Lack of Designated Operational Entities (DOEs)

So far, 29 companies have been accredited by the UNFCCC as DOEs, they play the crucial role of validating each and every project prior to submission for registration by the CDM EB, and of periodically verifying the emission reductions generated prior to their certification. Due to the significant entry barriers, in particular with regard to liability insurance requirements and the need for a track record in auditing across several sectors, there are no indigenous DOEs from India, although around 7 of the international firms have a presence in the Indian market, depending on how "presence" is defined.

Nevertheless, the number of accredited DOEs in India is already a constraint, and given the number of projects in the pipeline, this constraint will soon have an impact on transaction costs and liquidity as the market expands.

4.3.9 Lack of Capacity

Although there are a number of workshops and events that have served to raise awareness of the CDM and the opportunity provided by carbon finance, there remains a skills shortage for the development and delivery of CDM projects in India. So far, there are no courses offered by vocational or technical schools on carbon finance, and the best way to learn how to develop a project remains the learning-by-doing approach. The lack of expertise to identify carbon finance opportunities and develop the carbon asset remains an important barrier to the carbon market in India.

Chapter-5

Conclusion

There is widespread belief now that forests can be used to reduce the costs of slowing climate change. While the role of forests in the global carbon cycle has long been acknowledged, recent discussions within the context of the United Nations Framework Convention on Climate Change, as well as efforts to write climate change legislation in the United States, have emphasized the role forests might play. The most recent policy efforts have focused on near-term actions to reduce deforestation in tropical countries. The rationale for considering forests at all in the policy mix stems partly from the physical components of the issue. The world's forest estate is exceedingly large: It contains roughly 3.9 billion hectares of forestland and 1 trillion tons1 of CO_2 (UN Food and Agricultural Organization, 2006). Current estimates indicate that roughly 11 million hectares each year are lost in tropical regions due to deforestation and conversion of land to agriculture (Houghton, 1999, 2003). These losses cause emissions of about 3.6-4.5 billion tons of CO_2, so that deforestation accounts for around 17% of global carbon emissions. Countries like Indonesia and Brazil are near the top of total emissions when estimated by country if deforestation is included in carbon emission calculations. Efforts to slow these emissions, of course, could have enormous benefits for society.

Afforestation has been the most widely recognized and studied option for mitigation using forests to date. Afforestation refers to taking agricultural land and converting it into forests. Because agricultural land stores very little carbon in aboveground biomass, converting the land to trees, and allowing those trees to grow, will remove carbon from the atmosphere. A forest that is growing can remove 5-11 tons CO_2 per hectare per year, depending on location and productivity. A large proportion of the world's crop and grazing lands are rain-fed, indicating that they also can support trees. As a result, there are many opportunities to sequester carbon by converting this agricultural land into forests.Of course, converting land from agriculture to forests comes with a cost. Afforestation requires implementation and management costs, as well opportunity costs. Depending on the region, tree species, labor costs, site quality and other factors, planting and managing trees may cost $700 to more than $3000 per hectare in present value terms. As noted above, opportunity costs associated with converting land from agricultural uses to forest will also be important, and they will depend on the value of the land in agricultural production. The costs are important, but it is also important to recognize that there may be future benefits to planting trees. That is, because afforestation ultimately leads to standing forest stocks with potentially valuable timber, there may be some future benefits that can reduce the costs.

Global efforts have been made to establish a global forest carbon sequestration policy as part to combat global warming. It begins by describing important categories to consider when measuring the costs of forestry carbon sequestration, including opportunity costs, implementation and management costs, other transactions costs and system-wide costs (e.g., leakage or impacts in other markets). The current study indicates that the three key forestry activities such as afforestation, forest management and reductions in emissions from deforestation—can sequester large quantities of carbon. Over the next 30 years, the upper limit of potential sequestration could be as much as 15 billion tons CO_2 at more than \$100 per ton CO_2. At \$30 per ton CO_2, it may be possible to obtain around 6.7 billion tons CO_2 per year, with around 40% of this arising from avoided deforestation, 31% from forest management activities, and the rest from afforestation. A global sequestration program really is global, with potential contributions from virtually every region of the world. The largest share of sequestration is derived from avoided deforestation, but the roles of forest management and afforestation cannot be discounted. Of course, it is also important to acknowledge that there will be difficulties associated with starting and running carbon sequestration programs. Measuring, monitoring and verification protocols must be established and implemented. People will have to learn how to sell their carbon credits onto a market and the prospects of carbon finance mechanism.

Project Design Document (PDD) Format for CDM A/R Project Activities

(CDM A/R PDD-Version 10)

Part-I : General information on the project design document form for A/R (CDM-AR-PDD), and the form for proposed new baseline and monitoring methodology for A/R (CDM-AR-NM)

1. These guidelines seek to assist project participants in completing the following documents:
   - Project Design Document form (CDM-AR-PDD);
   - Proposed New Baseline and Monitoring Methodology form (CDM-AR-NM).
2. The CDM-AR-PDD and CDM-AR-NM forms were developed by the clean development mechanism (CDM) Executive Board in conformity with the Modalities and procedures for afforestation and reforestation project activities under the clean development mechanism. (hereafter referred to as CDM A/R modalities and procedures). The CDM-AR-PDD form is defined in

Appendix B Project Design Document of the CDM A/R modalities and procedures and the CDM-AR-NM form is based on Appendix C Terms of reference for establishing guidelines on baselines and monitoring methodologies for afforestation and reforestation project activities under the CDM of the CDM A/R modalities and procedures.

3. If project participants wish to submit an afforestation or reforestation (hereafter referred as A/R) project activity (hereafter referred to as A/R CDM project activity) for validation and registration, they shall submit a fully completed CDM-AR-PDD.
4. If project participants wish to propose a new baseline and monitoring methodology for A/R they shall complete and submit the CDM-AR-NM and a draft CDM-AR-PDD with at least the section. Application of an approved baseline and monitoring methodology (including relevant annexes) completed as draft, providing an example of the application of the A/R PNM.
5. The CDM-AR-PDD and CDM-AR-NM forms may be obtained electronically from the UNFCCC CDM website <http://cdm.unfccc.int>, by e-mail (cdm-info@unfccc.int) or in printed format from the UNFCCC secretariat (Fax: +49-228-815-1999).
6. Terms, which are underlined with a broken line in the CDM-AR-PDD and the CDM-AR-NM, are explained in the Glossary of CDM Terms, available on the CDM UNFCCC website. It is recommended that before or during the completion of the forms that project participants consult the most recent version of the Glossary of CDM Terms.
7. Project participants should also consult the section Guidance Clarifications available on the UNFCCC CDM website.
8. The CDM Executive Board (the Board) may revise the forms CDM-AR-PDD and CDM-AR-NM, if necessary.

9. Revisions to the form CDM-AR-PDD do not affect A/R project activities:
   (a) Already validated, or already submitted to the DOE for validation prior to the adoption of the revised CDM-AR-PDD;
   (b) Submitted to the DOEs within six months of the adoption of the revised CDM-AR PDD.
10. Revisions to the form CDM-AR-NM do not affect new baseline and monitoring methodology:
    (a) Submitted to the DOEs prior to the adoption of the revised CDM-AR-NM;
    (b) Submitted to the DOEs within six months of the adoption of the revised CDM-AR-NM.
11. The CDM-AR-PDD and CDM-AR-NM templates shall not be altered, that is, shall be completed using the same font without modifying its format, font, headings or logo.
12. Tables and their columns shall not be modified or deleted, rows may however be added, as needed.
13. If a section of the CDM-AR-PDD and CDM-AR-NM is not applicable, it shall be explicitly stated that the section is left blank on purpose.

Part II : Project design document for afforestation and regorestation project activities

A. Information note on Project Design Document for afforestation and reforestation project activities (CDM-AR-PDD)

1. The CDM-AR-PDD presents information on the essential technical and organizational aspects of the afforestation or reforestation (A/R) project activity and is a key input into the validation, registration and verification of the project as required under the Kyoto Protocol to the UNFCCC. The relevant modalities and procedures are

detailed in Decision 3/CMP.1 and Decision 5/CMP.1 of the Conference of the Parties serving as the meeting of the Parties to the Kyoto Protocol.

2. The CDM-AR-PDD contains information on the proposed A/R CDM project activity, and the approved baseline and monitoring methodology applied to the proposed A/R CDM project activity. It discusses and justifies the choice of baseline methodology and the applied monitoring plan, including monitoring of data and calculation methods.

3. Project participants (PPs) should submit the completed CDM-AR-PDD, together with attachments if necessary, to a designated operational entity for validation. The designated operational entity then examines the adequacy of the information provided in the CDM-AR-PDD, especially to check if it satisfies the relevant modalities and procedures. Based on this examination, the designated operational entity makes a decision regarding validation of the project.

4. Bearing in mind paragraph 6 of the CDM modalities and procedures, PPs shall submit documentation that contains confidential/proprietary information in two versions:

   - One marked up version where all confidential/proprietary parts shall be made illegible by the PPs (e.g. by covering those parts with black ink) so that this can be made publicly available;

   - A second version containing all information that shall be treated as strictly confidential by all handling this documentation (DOEs/AEs, Board members and alternates, panel/committee and working group members, external experts requested to consider such documents in support of work for the Board, and the secretariat).

B. Specific guidelines for completing the Project Design Document for afforestation and reforestation project activities (CDM-AR-PDD)

Contents

Section A : General description of the proposed A/R CDM project activity

A.1. Title of the proposed A/R CDM project activity

Please indicate

- ❐ The title of the A/R CDM project activity;
- ❐ The version number of the document;
- ❐ The date of the document.

A.2. Description of the proposed A/R CDM project activity

Please include in the description

- ❐ The purpose of the proposed A/R CDM project activity;
- ❐ Explain how the proposed project activity is undertaken e.g. what is being done and by whom;
- ❐ The view of the PPs on the contribution of the proposed A/R CDM project activity to sustainable development (max. one page).

A.3. Project participants

Please list PPs and Party(ies) involved and provide contact information in Annex 1. Information shall be indicated using the following tabular format.

Name of the Party involved* (Host indicates a host party)	Private and/ or public entity(ies) project participants* (as applicable)	Kindly indicate if Party involved wishes to be considered as project participant (Yes/No)
Name A	Private Entity A Public Entity A...	No
Name B	None	Yes
Name C	None	No

(*) In accordance with the A/R CDM modalities and procedures, at the time of making the CDM-AR-PDD public at the stage of validation, a Party involved may or may not have provided its approval. At the time of requesting registration, the approval by the Party(ies) involved is required.

Note: When the CDM-AR-PDD is prepared to support a proposed new baseline and monitoring methodology (form CDM-AR-NM), at least the host Party(ies) and any known project participant (e.g. those proposing a new methodology) shall be identified.

A.4. Description of location and boundaries of the A/R CDM project activity

A.4.1. Location of the proposed A/R CDM project activity

A.4.1.1. Host Party (ies)

A.4.1.2. Region/State/Province

A.4.1.3. City/Town/Community (if applicable)

A.4.2 Detailed geographic delineation of the project boundary, including information allowing the unique identification(s) of the proposed A/R CDM project activity

The project boundary geographically delineates the A/R CDM project activity under the control of the PPs.

The A/R CDM project activity may contain more than one discrete areas of land. If an A/R CDM project activity contains more than one discrete areas of land:

- Each discrete area of land should have a unique geographical identification;
- The boundary should be defined for each discrete area and should not include the areas in between these discrete areas of land.

A.5. Technical description of the A/R CDM project activity:

A.5.1. Concise description of the present environmental conditions of the area planned for the proposed A/R CDM project activity, including

A.5.1.1. Climate

A.5.1.2. Hydrology

A.5.1.3. Soils

A.5.1.4. Ecosystems

A.5.2. Description of the presence, if any, of rare and endangered species and their habitats

A.5.3. Species and varieties selected for the proposed A/R CDM project activity

A.5.4. Technology to be employed by the proposed A/R CDM project activity

This section should include a description of the environmentally safe and sustainable/technologies and know-how which will be employed by the PPs, as well as other technical information that may be used to assess the applicability of the selected baseline and monitoring methodology to the proposed A/R CDM project activity.

A.5.5. Transfer of technology/know-how, if applicable

This section should include a description of the technologies and know-how which will be transferred to the host Party(ies).

A.6. Description of legal title to the land, current land tenure and rights to tCERs/lCERs issued for the proposed A/R CDM project activity

This section should include a short description (or list) of legal title/s to the land, current land tenure and rights. It should allow determination of the owner of the tCERs/lCERs issued for the proposed A/R CDM project activity.

A.7. Assessment of the eligibility of the land

Please demonstrate that each discrete area of land to be included in the boundary is eligible for an A/R CDM project activity following the requirements of the applied methodology.

A.8. Approach for addressing non-permanence

In accordance with paragraph 38 and Section K of the CDM A/R modalities and procedures, please specify which of the following approaches to address non-permanence has been selected:

- ❒ Issuance of tCERs;
- ❒ Issuance of lCERs.

A.9. Estimated amount of net anthropogenic GHG removals by sinks over the chosen crediting period

Summary of results obtained in C.7., D.1., and D.2.

Year	Estimation of Baseline net GHG removals by sinks (tonnes of CO_2e)	Estimation of actual net GHG removals by sinks (tones of CO_2e)	Estimation of Leakage (tones of CO_2e)	Estimation of net anthropogenic GHG removals by sinks (tones of CO_2e)
Year A				
Year B				
Year C				
Year…				
Total t CO_2e				

A.10. Public funding of the proposed A/R CDM project activity

In case public funding from Parties included in Annex I is involved, please provide in Annex 2 information on sources of public funding for the project activity from Parties included in Annex I which shall provide an affirmation that such funding does not result in a diversion of official development assistance and is separate from and is not counted towards the financial obligations of those Parties.

Section B : Duration of the project activity/ crediting period

B.1 Starting date of the proposed A/R CDM project activity and of the crediting period

The starting date of an A/R CDM project activity is the date on which the implementation of an A/R CDM project activity begins. Please justify the starting date and provide any relevant documentation. Note that the crediting period starts at the starting date of the project activity.

Please note that the Board, at its twenty-first meeting, clarified that provisions of paragraphs 12 and 13 of decision 3/CMP.1 do not apply to A/R CDM project activities. An A/R CDM project activity starting after 1 January 2000 can also be validated and registered after 31 December 2005 as long as the first verification of the project activity occurs after the date of registration of this project activity. Given that the crediting period starts at the same date as the starting date of the project activity, the projects starting 2000 onwards can accrue tCERs / lCERs as of the starting date.

B.2. Expected operational lifetime of the proposed A/R CDM project activity

Please state the expected operational lifetime of the proposed A/R CDM project activity in years and months as appropriate.

B.3 Choice of crediting period

Please state whether the proposed A/R CDM project activity will use a renewable or a fixed crediting period and complete B.3.1. or B.3.2. Accordingly B.3.1. and B.3.2. are mutually exclusive . Please select only one of them

B.3.1. Length of the renewable crediting period (in years and months), if selected

Each crediting period shall be a maximum of 20 years and may be renewed at most two times, provided that, for each renewal, a designated operational entity determines and informs the Board that the original project baseline is still valid or has been updated taking account of new data where applicable. Please state whether the renewable crediting period is selected. If yes, please state the length of the crediting period in years and months.

B.3.2. Length of the fixed crediting period (in years and months), if selected

The fixed crediting period shall be at most 30 years. Please state whether the fixed crediting period is selected. If yes, please state the length of the crediting period in years and months.

Section C : Application of an approved baseline and monitoring methodology

C.1. Title and reference of the approved baseline and monitoring methodology applied to the proposed A/R CDM project activity

Please refer to the UNFCCC CDM website for the title and reference number of selected approved baseline and monitoring methodology.

1. Please indicate

- ❒ The approved A/R methodology and the version of the methodology that is used (e.g. AR-AM0001 - Version 02.);
- ❒ Any methodologies or tools which the approved methodology draws upon and their version (e.g. The tool for demonstration and assessment of additionality - Version 01.).

Note : The selected approved baseline and monitoring methodology becomes an integral part of the CDM-AR-PDD. There is no need to repeat the methodology in the CDM-AR-

PDD. Please refer to the methodology via heading and section number, equation number, table number, etc. Where PPs wish to propose a new baseline and monitoring methodology, please complete the form - Proposed New Baseline and Monitoring Methodology for A/R: (CDM-AR-NM) in accordance with the procedures for submission and consideration of proposed new methodologies. If a new baseline and monitoring methodology is proposed, please complete the form for Proposed New Baseline and Monitoring Methodology for A/R (CDM-AR-NM).

C.2. Assessment of the applicability of the selected approved methodology to the proposed A/R CDM project activity and justification of the choice of the methodology

Use this section to show that the proposed AR CDM project activity meets each of the applicability conditions of the selected methodology. Justify that the characteristics of the project (i.e. the specific way of site preparation, species composition of planted trees, displacement of certain types of pre-project activities) match appropriately with the approaches in the selected approved methodology in terms of availability of data, models/approaches used to estimate changes of carbon stocks. Justify and document the rationales and assumptions in a transparent manner. Explain which documentation has been used to support the justification and provide the references to the documentation or include the documentation as an annex.

C.3. Description of strata identified using the ex ante stratification

Describe results of application of the ex ante stratification procedure as provided in the selected approved methodology. Do not copy the ex ante stratification procedure to the PDD.

C.4. Identification of the baseline scenario (if the Combined Tool to identify the baseline scenario and demonstrate additionality in A/R CDM project activities. Is applied proceed to paragraph C.6)

Where the applied methodology requires use of the Combined tool to identify the baseline scenario and demonstrate additionality in A/R CDM project activities. Description of the identified baseline scenario for each stratum and assessment of additionality may be presented in Section C.6 and this section can be left blank.

C.4.1. Description of the application of the approach to identify the most plausible baseline scenario (separately for each stratum defined in C.3.)

Describe how the selected approved methodology is applied in order to identify the baseline scenario. Where the procedure involves several steps, describe how each step is applied and transparently document the outcome of each step. Explain and justify key assumptions and rationales. Provide relevant documentation or references. Illustrate in a transparent manner all data used to determine baseline scenarios (variables, parameters, data sources, etc), preferably in a tabular form. You may wish to refer to the information provided in Section A of this document. Do not copy the information from Section A here.

C.4.2. Description of the identified baseline scenario (separately for each stratum defined in Section C.3.)

Describe the most plausible baseline scenario for each stratum, as resulting from the application of the procedures to identify the baseline scenario.

C.5. Assessment and demonstration of additionality (if the Combined tool to identify the baseline scenario and demonstrate additionality in A/R CDM project activities is not used)

Describe the application of the procedure to assess and demonstrate additionality according to the selected approved baseline and monitoring methodology. Where the procedure involves several steps, describe how each step is applied and transparently document the outcome of each step. Explain and justify key assumptions and rationales. Provide relevant documentation or references. Illustrate in a transparent manner all data used to determine baseline scenarios (variables, parameters, data sources, etc), preferably in a table form. Compare the baseline scenario as identified above against the project scenario. Use (refer to) information provided e.g. in Section A. Show that the project scenario could not happen in absence of the A/R CDM project activity.

If the starting date of the project activity is before the date of validation, provide evidence that the incentive from the CDM was seriously considered in the decision to proceed with the project activity. This evidence shall be based on (preferably official, legal and/or other corporate) documentation that was, available at, or prior to, the start of the project activity.

C.6. Identification of the baseline scenario and demonstration of additionality using the combined tool to identify the baseline scenario and demonstrate additionality in A/R CDM project activities. (if required by the selected approved methodology)

Describe the application of the .Combined tool to identify the baseline scenario and demonstrate additionality in A/R CDM project activities. Describe how each step is applied and transparently document the outcome of each step. Explain and justify key assumptions and rationales. Provide relevant documentation or references. Illustrate in a transparent manner all data used to determine baseline scenarios (variables, parameters, data sources, etc), preferably in a table form.

C.7. Estimation of the ex ante baseline net GHG removals by sinks

Calculate the ex ante baseline net GHG removals by sinks for the chosen crediting period using the approach provided in the selected approved baseline and monitoring methodology. Use a stepwise approach and name components being calculated. List numerical values and sources of all data used in the above calculation (use table provided below). Data and parameters that is available at validation

(Copy this table for each data and parameter)

Data / Parameter
Description/ unit:
Value applied:
Source of data:
Justification of choice / Measurement procedures (if any):
Any Comments:

Years	**Annual estimation of net anthropogenic GHG removals by sinks in tones of CO_2 - equivalent (CO_2e)**
Year A	
Year B	
Year C	
Year…	
Total estimated net anthropogenic GHG removals by sinks (tonnes of CO_2e)	
Total no. of crediting years	
Annual average over the crediting period of estimated net anthropogenic GHG removals by sinks (tonnes of CO_2e)	

Section D : Estimation of ex ante actual net GHG removals by sinks, leakage, and estimated amount of net anthropogenic GHG removals by sinks over the chosen crediting period

D.1. Estimate of the ex ante actual net GHG removals by sinks

The actual net GHG removals by sinks is the sum of verifiable changes in carbon stocks, minus the increase in emissions of the GHGs measured in units of CO2 equivalent by the sources that are increased as result of the implementation of the proposed A/R CDM project activity within the project boundary. Calculate the ex ante actual net GHG removals by sinks for the chosen crediting period using the approach provided in the selected approved baseline and monitoring methodology . Use a stepwise approach and name components being calculated. List numerical values and sources of all data used in the above calculation. Refer to, but do not copy, pieces of the selected approved methodology, unless necessary.

D.2. Estimate of the ex ante leakage

Leakage is defined as: the increase of anthropogenic emissions by sources of GHG which occurs outside the project boundary and that is measurable and attributable to the proposed A/R CDM project activity. Calculate the ex ante leakage for the chosen crediting period using the approach provided in the selected approved baseline and monitoring methodology (annually, for each gas, pool, source, in units of CO2 equivalent). Use a stepwise approach and name components being calculated. List numerical values and sources of all data used in the above calculation. Refer to, but do not copy, pieces of the selected approved methodology, unless necessary.

Section E : Monitoring plan

E.1. Monitoring of the project implementation

E.1.1. Monitoring of forest establishment and management if required for the compliance with the applicability conditions of the selected approved methodology

Please list data that shall be collected during monitoring of forest establishment and management. If applicable, refer to data dealt with in other sections of the monitoring plan. Please state if not applicable.

E.1.2. Information on how geographic coordinates of the project boundary are established, recorded and archived

Describe how the geographic coordinates of the project boundary, including boundaries of strata if any, are determined and recorded. Present the data in a tabular form. If the data is so voluminous as to occupy a large space on paper the same can be reported in electronic form. If so, include a description of the electronic database/format being used for this purpose.

E.1.3. If required by the selected approved methodology, describe, or provide reference to, SOPs and quality control (QC) and quality assurance (QA) procedures undertaken for data monitored, if not included in the relevant sections below:

E.2. Sampling design and stratification

Describe application of the ex post stratification procedure as provided in the selected approved baseline and monitoring methodology. Do not copy and paste the above-mentioned section. If stratification, as required in this section is identical to that provided in Section C.4. of the PDD, it is sufficient to refer to it.

E.3. Monitoring of the baseline net GHG removals by sinks, if required by the selected approved methodology

Please state if monitoring of the baseline net GHG removals by sinks is required by the selected approved baseline and monitoring methodology. If not, skip Sections E.3.1. and E.3.2. Data and parameters that are monitored (if any):

Data / Parameter:
Description/ unit:
Source of Data
Measurement procedures
Monitoring frequency
QA/QC frequency
Any Comments:

E.4. Monitoring of the actual net GHG removals by sinks

Please provide a description of data and parameters used in monitoring of actual net GHG removals by sinks. Use the tabular format provided below.

Data and parameters that is available at validation

Data / Parameter:
Description/ unit:
Value applied:
Source of data:
Justification of choice / Measurement procedures (if any):
Any Comments:

Data and parameters that are monitored

Data / Parameter:
Description/ unit:
Source of Data
Measurement procedures
Monitoring frequency
QA/QC frequency
Any Comments:

E.5. Leakage

Please state if monitoring of leakage is required by the selected approved baseline and monitoring methodology. Please provide a description of data and parameters used in estimation/monitoring of leakage. Use the tabular format provided below.

Data and parameters that is available at validation

Data / Parameter:	
Description/unit:	
Value applied:	
Source of data:	
Justification of choice / Measurement procedures (if any):	
Any Comments:	

Data and parameters that are monitored

Data / Parameter:
Description/ unit:
Source of Data
Measurement procedures
Monitoring frequency
QA/QC frequency
Any Comments:

E.5.1. Proposed measures to be implemented to minimize potential leakage

E.5.2. Specify the procedures for the periodic review of implementation of activities and measures to minimize leakage, if required by the selected approved methodology

E.6. Provide any additional quality control (QC) and quality assurance (QA) procedures undertaken for data monitored not included in section E.1.3.

Data (Indicate ID number)	**Uncertainty level of data (High/Medium/Low)**	**Explain QA/QC procedures planned for these data, or why such procedures are not necessary**

E.7. Please describe the operational and management structure(s) that the project operator will implement in order to monitor actual GHG removals by sinks and any leakage generated by the proposed A/R CDM project activity:

Section F : Environmental impacts of the proposed A/R CDM project activity

F.1. Documentation on the analysis of the environmental impacts, including impacts on biodiversity and natural ecosystems, and impacts outside the project boundary of the proposed A/R CDM project activity

This analysis should include, where applicable, information on impacts on, inter alia, hydrology, soils, risk of fires, pests and diseases. Please attach the relevant documentation to the CDM-AR-PDD.

F.2. If any negative impact is considered significant by the project participants or the host Party, a statement that project participants have undertaken an environmental impact assessment, in accordance with the procedures required by the host Party, including conclusions and all references to support documentation

Please attach the documentation to the CDM-AR-PDD (if applicable).

F.3. Description of planned monitoring and remedial measures to address significant impacts referred to in section F.2. above

Section G : Socio-economic impacts of the proposed A/R CDM project activity

G.1. Documentation on the analysis of the major socio-economic impacts, including impacts outside the project boundary of the proposed A/R CDM project activity

This analysis should include, where applicable, information on impacts on, inter alia, local communities, indigenous peoples, land tenure, local employment, food production, cultural and religious sites and access to fuelwood and other forest products. Please attach the documentation to the CDM-AR-PDD.

G.2. If any negative impact is considered significant by the project participants or the host Party, a statement that project participants have undertaken a socio-economic impact assessment, in accordance with the procedures required by the host Party, including conclusions and all references to supporting documentation

Please attach the documentation to the CDM-AR-PDD (if applicable).

G.3. Description of planned monitoring and remedial measures to address significant impacts referred to in section G.2. above

Section H : Stakeholders comments

H.1. Brief description of how comments by local stakeholders have been invited and compiled

Please describe the process by which comments by local stakeholders have been invited and compiled. An invitation for comments by local stakeholders shall be made in an open and transparent manner, in a way that facilitates comments to be received from local stakeholders and allows for a reasonable time for comments to be submitted. In this regard, PPs shall describe an A/R CDM project activity in a manner which allows the local stakeholders to understand the proposed A/R CDM project activity, taking into account confidentiality provisions of the CDM modalities and procedures.

H.2. Summary of the comments received

Please identify stakeholders that have made comments and provide a summary of these comments.

H.3. Report on how due account was taken of any comments received

Please explain how due account have been taken of comments received from stakeholders.

Annexure-1 : Contact Information on Participants in the Proposed A/R CDM Project Activity

Organization

Street/P.O. box

Building

City

State/Region

Postfix/ZIP

Country

Telephone

Fax

E-Mail

URL

Represented by

Title

Salutation

Last Name

Middle Name

First Name

Department

Mobile

Direct Fax

Personal e-mail

Direct tel

Annexure-2 : Information Regarding Public Funding

Please provide information from Parties included in Annex 1(above) on sources of public funding for the proposed A/R CDM project activity, which shall provide an affirmation that such funding does not result in a diversion of official development assistance and is separate from and is not counted towards the financial obligations of those Parties.

Annexure-3 : Baseline Information

Annex 3 shall provide any relevant information not included in Section C or in the selected approved baseline and monitoring methodology. Please state if Annex 3 is left intentionally blank.

Annexure-4 : Monitoring Plan

Please provide any further background information used in the application of the monitoring methodology. This may include tables with time series data, additional documentation of measurement procedures, etc.

Part III : Form for proposed new baseline and monitoring methodology for afforestation and reforestation

A. Information note on form for Proposed New Methodology for afforestation and reforestation project activities (CDM-AR-NM)

1. Before considering the proposal of a new baseline and monitoring methodology, the list of approved A/R methodologies should be checked by the PPs to verify whether an approved baseline and monitoring methodology could be used, with or without revision, for the proposed project activity. In case modifications are required, please refer to the guidance provided by the Board on criteria for the consolidation and revision of the approved methodologies (EB 27, Annex 10) and guidance on when to request a revision, clarification or deviation to an approved methodology (EB 31, Annex 12). This guidance is available at <http://cdm.unfccc.int/EB/index.html>.

2. The form proposed new baseline and monitoring methodology for A/R. (CDM-AR-NM) is to be used to propose a new baseline methodology and a new monitoring methodology. The most recent version of this form may be obtained from the forms section of the UNFCCC CDM website <http://cdm.unfccc.int> or from the UNFCCC secretariat by e-mail (cdm-info@unfccc.int) or in print via fax (+49-228-815-1999).

3. The form proposed new baseline and monitoring methodology for A/R. (CDM-AR NM) shall be

accompanied by a Project Design Document for A/R. (CDM-AR-PDD) with at least the section .Application of an approved baseline and monitoring methodology (including relevant annexes) completed as draft, providing an example of the application of the A/R PNM.

4. The form proposed new baseline and monitoring methodology for A/R. (CDM-AR-NM) shall be submitted to the Board in accordance with .Procedure for the submission and consideration of requests for revision of approved baseline and monitoring methodologies and tools for A/R CDM project activities.
5. Each proposed new baseline and monitoring methodology should use a separate form proposed new baseline and monitoring methodology for A/R. (CDM-AR-NM). .Proposed new baseline and monitoring methodology for A/R. (CDM-AR-NM) forms for several new baselines and monitoring methodologies may be submitted together with the same CDM-AR-PDD for several components of a proposed project activity.
6. For additional guidance on aspects to be covered in the description of a new methodology, please refer to guidance and clarifications by the Board on the guidance clarifications section of the UNFCCC CDM website6 and the Glossary of CDM Terms. PPs are encouraged to use, as appropriate and to the extent possible, the Intergovernmental Panel on Climate Change (IPCC) Good Practice Guidance (GPG) for Land Use, Land-Use Change and Forestry (LULUCF).
7. PPs shall refrain from employing key terminology not used in the documents of the Conference of the Parties (COP) or the Glossary of CDM Terms and refrain from rewriting the instructions on the forms.

8. The methodology procedure shall:

   (a) Be completed in a fashion that can be readily used as an approved methodology. This requires use of appropriate format, tone and level of specificity. Text shall be clear and succinct, well written and logically sequenced. It shall describe the procedures in a manner that is sufficiently explicit to enable the methodology to be carried out by a methodology user, to be applied to projects unambiguously and reproduced by a third party. It shall be possible for projects following the methodology to be subjected to a validation and/or verification study. Methodology developers should review and be familiar with methodologies approved by the Board;

   (b) Be generally appropriate for the entire group of project activities that satisfy the specified applicability conditions. A new methodology should therefore stand independently from the specific project activity proposed in the draft CDM-AR-PDD with which the new methodology is being submitted. The methodology should not make direct reference to, or depend on characteristics of, the specific project activity being proposed in the draft CDM-AR-PDD. It should not refer to specific project activities or locations, project-specific conditions or project-specific parameters. This project-specific information should be described in the draft CDM-AR-PDD however; it can be referred to in the explanation/justification section to help describe the methodology;

   (c) Present the methodology steps as one might present a recipe. In doing so, clearly state what the methodology user must do and what information must be presented in the resulting CDM-AR-PDD. It should include all algorithms, formulae, and step-by-step procedures needed to apply the methodology and validate the project activity, i.e. calculating baseline removals, project removals and leakage emissions. The completed form shall provide standalone replicable methodologies, and avoid reference to any secondary documents other than EB-approved tools and methodologies;

(d) Indicate precisely what information the project proponent must report in the draft CDM-AR-PDD and/or in monitoring reports;

(e) Support important procedures and concepts with equations and diagrams. Non-essential information should be avoided;

(f) Refer by name and reference number to approved methodologies and tools if they are used in whole or in part in the methodology. Relevant sections can be cited specifically, but do not need to be repeated. Any proposed modifications and/or additions to approved tools and methodologies need to be clearly highlighted. PPs are encouraged to use, to the extent feasible, the tools approved by the Board. The approved A/R methodological tools are available on the UNFCCC website

(g) Specify, for all formulae/algorithms and/or models:

❐ The variables used (e.g. species, tree density, growth rates);

❐ The spatial resolution of data (e.g. local, regional, national, etc.);

❐ The vintage of data.

(h) Use common formats for equations and terms and use international system of units (SI units);

(i) Specify, for the data sources and assumptions:

❐ Where the data are obtained from (official statistics, expert judgment, proprietary data, IPCC GPG for

LULUCF, commercial data and scientific literature, etc.);

- The assumptions used, if any.

(j) Clearly specify data requirements and sources, as well as procedures to be followed if expected data are unavailable. For instance, the methodology could point to a preferred data source (e.g. national statistics for the past five years), and indicate a priority order for use of additional data (e.g. using longer time series) and/or fall back data sources when the preferred sources are not available (e.g. corporate sources, international statistics, etc.);

(k) Include instructions to assist in implementing the methodology in a conservative manner where logical or quantitative assumptions have to be made by the methodology user, particularly in cases of uncertainty.

10. The explanation and justification sections shall:

(a) Be used to assist the assessment by the A/R WG and the Board in reviewing the methodology. If the proposed methodology is approved these sections are removed from the final version;

(b) Provide the rationale for the procedures presented;

(c) If the procedure draws from an approved methodology or tool, provide reference of the same and clearly note any changes to them or elaborations of them. Justify why such changes have been made;

(d) Point out the key logical and quantitative assumptions, i.e. those assumptions to which the results of the baseline methodology are particularly sensitive;

(e) Be clear about sources of uncertainty. Clearly point out which logical or quantitative assumptions have significant uncertainty associated with determining them. If the methodology makes a certain assumption in cases where there is uncertainty, explain why this assumption is appropriate;

(f) Explain how the methodology ensures conservativeness. Explain how the procedures and assumptions on which the procedures rely are conservative. In particular, explain how assumptions in the case of uncertainty are conservative.

11. General instructions for completing the baseline methodology section of the new methodology form (CDM-AR-NM):

(a) The baseline for an A/R CDM project activity is the scenario that reasonably represents the sum of the changes in carbon stocks in the carbon pools within the project boundary that would occur in the absence of the proposed A/R CDM project activity. A baseline shall cover all carbon pools within the project boundary, but PPs may choose not to account for one or more carbon pools if they provide transparent and verifiable information showing that the carbon stock in the pool under project scenario will not decrease relative to the baseline scenario. The general characteristics of a baseline are contained in paragraphs 20 to 22 of the CDM A/R modalities and procedures;

(b) When drafting a proposed new baseline methodology, PPs shall, in particular, follow the following steps:

(i) Choose and justify which one of the baseline approaches listed in paragraph 22 of the CDM A/R modalities and procedures is considered to be the most appropriate;

(ii) Elaborate a proposal for a new baseline methodology. A baseline methodology is an application of the selected baseline approach contained in paragraphs 22 (a) to (c) of the CDM A/R modalities and procedures to an individual A/R

CDM project activity, reflecting aspects such as sector, technology and region. The Board agreed that no methodology is to be excluded a priori so that PPs have the opportunity to propose any methodology, which they consider appropriate. The PPs shall take into account guidance by the Board on aspects to be covered by a methodology (please see guidance and clarifications by the Board on the Guidance clarifications web page of the UNFCCC CDM website);

(iii) Describe the proposed new methodology using the form for Proposed New Methodology for A/R. (CDM-AR-NM) taking into account guidance given by the Board as well as the information provided in the CDM-AR-PDD;

(iv) Demonstrate the applicability of the proposed methodology, and, implicitly, that of the approach, to an A/R CDM project activity by providing relevant information in the section .Application of an approved baseline and monitoring methodology of a draft CDM-AR-PDD;

(c) In accordance with guidance provided by the Board, the proposed new baseline methodology shall include a basis for determining the baseline scenario and, in particular:

(i) An explanation of how the baseline scenario is chosen, taking into account paragraph 20 (e) of the A/R modalities and procedures;

(ii) An underlying rationale for algorithm/formulae and/or model used in the baseline methodology;

(iii) An explanation of how, through the methodology, it is demonstrated that a proposed A/R CDM project activity is additional and, therefore, not the baseline scenario (to be used in Section C.5 or C.6 of the CDM-AR-PDD);

(iv) Delineation of the project boundary.

12. General instructions for completing the monitoring methodology section of the new methodology form (CDM-AR-NM):

    (a) Monitoring of an A/R CDM project activity refers to the collection and archiving of all relevant data necessary for determining the baseline net GHG removals by sinks, measuring actual net GHG removals by sinks within the project boundary of an A/R CDM project activity, leakage and applicability conditions, as applicable;

    (b) When drafting a proposed new monitoring methodology, PPs shall:

        (i) Describe the proposed new methodology using the form proposed new baseline and monitoring methodology for A/R. (CDM-AR-NM) taking into account guidance given by the Board;

        (ii) Demonstrate the applicability of the proposed monitoring methodology to an A/R CDM project activity by providing relevant information in sections of a draft CDM-AR-PDD.

    (c) The monitoring methodology needs to provide detailed information on how to establish the monitoring plan related to the collection and archiving of all relevant data needed to:

        (i) Estimate or measure actual net GHG removals by sinks occurring within the project boundary;

        (ii) Determine the baseline net GHG removals by sinks;

        (iii) Identify all potential sources of and estimate leakage for A/R CDM project activities.

    (d) The monitoring methodology should reflect good monitoring practice appropriate to the type of A/R CDM project activity.

13. PPs shall use the nomenclature for parameters and variables in the formulas, as found in recently approved A/R methodologies, when submitting proposed new methodologies.

B. Specific guidelines for A/R (CDM-AR-NM) proposed new baseline and monitoring methodology for A/R (CDM-AR-NM) (Version)

Contents

1. Methodology title and history of submission

Methodology title

History of submission (to be completed by the secretariat)

A/R WG recommendation (to be completed by the A/R WG)

(a) To approve this proposed A/R methodology as contained in an annex to the A/R WG meeting report;

(b) To reconsider this proposed A/R methodology, subject to required changes.
Major required changes;

Other required changes

(c) Not to approve the proposed A/R methodology. Reasons for non-approval;

Section I : Source, Definitions and Applicability

1. Sources

If this methodology is based on a previous submission or an approved methodology, please state the relevant reference number (ARNMXXXX/ AR-AMXXXX). Explain briefly the main differences and/or rationale for not using the approved methodology.

This methodology refers to the latest approved versions of the following procedures, tools, guidelines and guidance:

A/R WG assessment (to be completed by the A/R WG) Relationship with approved or pending A/R methodologies (if applicable).

(a) Does the proposed new A/R methodology include part(s) of one or more approved A/R methodology or an A/R methodology pending approval (see EB reports)? If so, please briefly note the relevant methodology reference numbers (AR-AMXXXX or ARNMXXXX), titles, and parts included;

(b) In particular, is the proposed new A/R methodology largely an amendment or extension of an approved A/R methodology? (i.e. the methodology largely consists of expanding an approved methodology to cover additional project contexts, applicability conditions, etc., and is thus largely comprised of text from an existing approved methodology);

(c) Please briefly note any significant differences or inconsistencies between the proposed new A/R methodology and approved A/R methodology (ies) of similar scope;

(d) To avoid potential repetition, feel free to provide one comprehensive answer here that covers question a) through c).

2. Selected baseline approach from paragraph 22 of the A/R CDM modalities and procedures: Choose one (delete others)

Existing or historical, as applicable, changes in carbon stocks in the carbon pools within the project boundary; Changes in carbon stocks in the carbon pools within the project boundary from a land use that represents an economically attractive course of action, taking into account barriers to investment; Changes in carbon stocks in the pools within the project boundary from the most likely land use at the time the project starts.

Explanation/justification of choice (if not self-explanatory)

3. Definitions

If needed, provide definitions of key new terms that are used in the proposed new methodology but are not defined in the Glossary of CDM Terms. To the maximum extent possible, use definitions from approved methodologies.

For the purpose of this methodology, the following specific definitions apply

Explanation/justification of choice of the definitions (if not self-explanatory)

4. Applicability

This methodology is applicable to the following type of project(s):

The conditions under which this methodology is applicable to A/R CDM project activities are:

List any conditions that a proposed AR CDM project activity must satisfy in order for the methodology to be applicable (e.g. eligible species, sectoral circumstances, region, or historical use of the land areas).Applicability conditions must pertain to the type of proposed project activity and prevent management practices that are not consistent with the carbon pools and sources selected or excluded. Applicability conditions should not be conditions on a presumed baseline scenario (e.g.

it is not appropriate for an applicability condition to be .The land area would continue to be the same without the project activity. as this is not a condition on the project activity, but a result of baseline assessment).In some cases, compliance with an applicability condition is obvious, easily validated, and unlikely to change. In other cases, however, compliance with an applicability condition may need to be monitored during the crediting period, and the consequences of non-compliance would need to be indicated in the methodology. For example, if an applicability condition is .The project activity does not result in the displacement of more than 50% of the pre-project activities., the methodology should explain how the applicability condition can be satisfied (e.g. through monitoring of displacements), and how it will be reported. Where applicable, provide references to the relevant sections of the proposed methodology which provide guidance on approaches required to check if the applicability conditions are satisfied.

Explanation/justification (if not self-explanatory)

Provide explanation/justification of the choices if the description is not self-explanatory. Provide references as necessary. Explain implicit and explicit key assumptions in a transparent manner.

A/R WG assessment (to be completed by the A/R WG)

(a) Please provide your assessment of the applicability conditions of the proposed new A/R CDM methodology. The language used in the description of the applicability conditions should follow the one used in the last version of approved A/R CDM methodologies and any differences shall reflect differences in the substance. If necessary, explain any changes that should be made to the applicability conditions;

(b) Please specify whether this methodology can be applied to other type of potential A/R CDM project activities;

(c) Indicate whether an approved methodology exists for the same applicability conditions;

(d) State whether the approach/language applied by project participants (PPs) follows to the maximum possible extent the one used in the approved A/R CDM methodologies and whether any differences reflect differences in the substance. If not, identify the inconsistencies.

Section II : Baseline Methodology Procedure

1. Project boundary and eligibility of land

The project boundary geographically delineates the afforestation or reforestation project activity under the control of the PPs. The A/R CDM project activity may contain more than one discrete area of land.

Each discrete area of land shall have a unique geographical identification. It shall be demonstrated that each discrete area of land to be included in the boundary is eligible for an A/R CDM project activity. PPs shall apply the latest version of the tool Procedures to demonstrate the eligibility of lands for afforestation and reforestation CDM project activities as approved by the Board. The latest version of Guidance on the application of the definition of project boundary to A/R CDM project activities (available at: <http://cdm.unfccc.int/Reference/Guidclarif>) may be applied in identification of areas of land planned for an A/R CDM project activity.

The carbon pools included in or excluded from the project boundary are shown in Table 1.

Table 1 : Selection and justification of carbon pools

Carbon Pools	Selected (answer with yes or no)	Justification
Aboveground trees		
Belowground trees		
Dead wood		
Forest floor (litter)		
Soil organic carbon		

The emission sources included in or excluded from the project boundary are shown in Table 2.

Table 2 : Sources of non-CO_2 greenhouse gases included in estimation of the actual net GHG removals by sinks and the leakage [add/delete gases and sources as needed]

Sources	Gas	Included/Excluded	Justification/Explanation of Choice
	CH_4		
	N_2O		

An emission sources can be neglected, i.e. accounted as zero, if the application of the most recent version of the .Tool for testing significance of GHG emissions in A/R CDM project activities leads to the conclusion that the emission source is insignificant.

Explanation/justification of choice (only if space in the tables above is not sufficient)

The project boundary geographically delineates the A/R CDM project activity under the control of the PPs.

The methodology shall contain the approach required to establish the geographical delineation of the project boundary for a proposed A/R CDM project activity.

The methodology shall explicitly state all carbon pools and emission sources included in the project boundary.

(a) Use Table 1 to list the carbon pools. Explain whether any carbon pools related to the baseline or the project activity have been excluded, and if so, justify their exclusion. Compare baseline and project if different;

(b) Use Table 2 to list the emission sources. Explain whether any emission sources have been excluded, and if so, justify their exclusion while making conservative assumptions.

A/R WG assessment (to be completed by the A/R WG)

(a) State whether the selection of carbon pools is appropriate in the context of the applicability conditions and the determination of actual net GHG removals by sinks and baseline net GHG removals by sinks. If not, explain the shortcomings and required changes. Note that the same carbon pools should be considered for the actual net GHG removals by sinks and baseline net GHG removals by sinks;

(b) State whether the selection of emissions by sources is appropriate taking into account the applicability conditions of the proposed A/R methodology.

2. Identification of the baseline scenario and demonstration of additionality

Methodology procedure

Provide a systematic, step-by-step procedure for determining the most likely baseline scenario. This procedure should describe a process for identifying the options to be considered as plausible candidate baseline scenarios. It should clearly explain the logical and analytical steps that must be followed in ascertaining the most likely baseline scenario from among these candidates. It should clearly state what the methodology user must do and what information must be presented in the resulting CDM-AR-PDD in order to make a logical and well-substantiated case for the baseline scenario. Be specific and complete, so that the procedure can be carried out in an unambiguous way, replicated, and subjected to a validation study. Ensure consistency between baseline scenario derived by this methodology and the procedure and formulae used to calculate the baseline net GHG removals by sinks (below). The baseline scenario determination procedure should indicate for which baseline scenarios the overall methodology is applicable. Explain why the proposed procedure for determining the baseline scenario is appropriate for the project type and applicability conditions. Justify that the range of options to be considered as plausible baseline scenarios is sufficiently comprehensive. The options to be considered should not exclude plausible options that, if included, might result in the determination of a different baseline scenario. Explain how national and/or sectoral policies and circumstances, if and as relevant, are taken into account by the methodology. Highlight the key logical assumptions and quantitative factors underlying the procedure for determining the baseline scenario. State clearly which assumptions and factors have significant uncertainty associated with them, and how such uncertainty is to be addressed. PPs may consider the use of the combined tool to identify the baseline scenario and demonstrate additionality as approved by the Board. Provide a systematic step-by-step procedure for determining whether or not the project activity is, or is a part of, the baseline scenario, and thereby determining whether the project activity is additional. The methodology should clearly state what the methodology user must do and what information must be presented in the resulting CDM-AR-PDD in order to make a logical and well-substantiated case for the project's additionality. Ensure consistency between baseline scenario derived by this methodology and the procedure and formulae used to demonstrate additionality. Note, for many methodologies there will be a strong link between the baseline scenario and additionality sections. Present the procedures in each step in as much detail as needed, but avoid repetition that is not needed for reasons of clarity. Highlight the key logical assumptions and quantitative factors underlying the procedure for demonstrating that the project activity is additional. State clearly which assumptions and factors have significant uncertainty associated with them, and how such uncertainty is to be addressed. If relevant, explain how national and/or sectoral policies and circumstances are taken into account by the methodology. PPs may consider the use of one of the tools approved by the Board: (i) Tool for the demonstration and assessment of additionality for afforestation and reforestation CDM project activities or (ii) Combined tool to identify the baseline scenario and demonstrate additionality.

Explanation/justification (if not self-explanatory)

A/R WG assessment (to be completed by the A/R WG)

(a) Explain whether the methodology provides for an appropriate step-wise procedure to identify the most plausible baseline scenario. Assess the appropriateness of this procedure, including the appropriateness of information to be presented in the resulting CDM-AR-PDD. Explain any shortcomings and list the required changes;

(b) Explain whether the methodology provides for an appropriate step-wise procedure for demonstration that the proposed A/R project activity is additional and therefore not the baseline scenario. Assess the appropriateness of this procedure, including the appropriateness of information to be presented in the resulting CDM-AR-PDD. Identify any shortcomings and list the required changes;

(c) State whether the procedure to demonstrate additionality is consistent with the procedure to identify the most plausible baseline scenario. If not, identify the inconsistencies;

(d) State whether the approach/language applied by PPs follows to the maximum possible extent the one used in the approved A/R CDM methodologies and whether any differences reflect differences in the substance. If not, identify the inconsistencies.

3. Stratification

If the project activity area is not homogeneous, stratification should be carried out to improve the accuracy and the precision of biomass estimates. Different stratifications may be required for the baseline and the project scenarios in order to achieve optimal accuracy of the estimates of net GHG removal by sinks.

Methodology procedure

Explanation/justification (if not self-explanatory)

A/R WG assessment (to be completed by the A/R WG

(a) Explain whether the methodology provides for an appropriate approach for stratification of the proposed A/R project activity. Identify any shortcomings and list the required changes;

(b) State whether the approach/language applied by PPs follows to the maximum possible extent the one used in the approved A/R CDM methodologies and whether any differences reflect differences in the substance. If not, identify the inconsistencies.

4. Baseline net GHG removals by sinks

Methodology procedure

Elaborate all algorithms and formulae used to estimate measure or calculate the baseline net GHG removals by sinks. Be specific and complete, so that the procedure can be carried out in an unambiguous way, replicated, and subjected to a validation study:

(a) Explain the underlying rationale for algorithm/formulae;

(b) Use consistent variables, equation formats, subscripts, etc.;

(c) Number all equations;

(d) Define all parameters, coefficients, variables, etc used in the equations, with units indicated;

(e) Justify the conservativeness of the approach applied.

If the methodology requires ex post determination of the baseline net GHG removals by sinks, provide a consistent step-by-step procedure. Elaborate all algorithms variables and formulae required. The ex post calculation of baseline net GHG removals by sinks may only be used if proper justification is provided. Notwithstanding this, the baseline net GHG removals by sinks shall also be calculated ex ante and reported in the draft CDM-PDD. For each of the parameters, coefficients, variables, etc, the methodology shall describe the basis for the values to be selected for these variables.

(a) Where values are provided in the methodology:

(i) Clearly indicate the precise references from which these values are taken (e.g. official statistics, IPCC Guidelines, commercial and scientific literature);

(ii) Justify the conservative application of the values provided.

(b) Where values are to be provided by the project participant, the methodology shall clearly indicate how the values are to be selected and justified:

(i) For variables that are not monitored throughout the project life time, but are derived from default values or one time measurements and remain fixed throughout crediting period, this shall be detailed in paragraph 8 of Section II;

(ii) For variables that are monitored, this shall be detailed in paragraph 3 of Section III.

Ensure consistency between the elaboration of the baseline scenario and the procedure for calculating the emissions of the baseline.

The Board has approved several A/R Methodological Tools. Please refer to the CDM website for these tools. The tools may be used whenever their applicability conditions allow. They should be used as stand-alone procedures, without changes, and need not be copied but only referenced in the proposed methodology. Make sure that the applicability conditions of the tool are met by the proposed project activity, the carbon pools and emission source referred to in the proposed methodology correspond to that in the tool, and that output of the tool and the methodology are consistent (e.g. with respect to units). Apart from using the existing approved tools, project proponents are also encouraged to propose new tools in areas where no tool exists or approved tools are not appropriate.

Explanation/justification (if not self-explanatory)

A/R WG assessment (to be completed by the A/R WG)

(a) State whether the methodology provides a complete approach for estimation of baseline net GHG removal by sinks. State whether the approach is appropriate and, if not, identify the shortcomings and list required changes;

(b) Provide an assessment of the appropriateness and correctness of the methodological procedure to calculate baseline net GHG removals by sinks, including an assessment of:

(i) The choice of algorithms/formulae and/or models used and correctness of their application (e.g. mathematical deficiencies, inconsistencies in calculus of dimensions);

(ii) The appropriateness (adequacy, consistency, accuracy and reliability) of the parameters used in the methodology;

(iii) State, whether the procedure results in a conservative estimation of the sum of the changes in carbon stocks in the carbon pools within the project boundary that would have occurred in the absence of the proposed A/R CDM project activity, taking into account the uncertainties associated with the data and parameters used. Assess whether the procedure can be carried out in an unambiguous way, replicated, and subjected to a validation and/or verification study.

Identify any shortcomings and list the required changes.

(c) State whether the approach/language applied by PPs follows to the maximum possible extent the one used in the approved A/R CDM methodologies and whether any differences reflect differences in the substance. If not, identify the inconsistencies.

5. Actual net GHG removals by sinks

Methodology procedure

Elaborate all algorithms and formulae used to estimate measure or calculate the removals and emissions from the project activity. Be specific and complete, so that the procedure can be carried out in an unambiguous way, replicated, and subjected to a validation and/or verification study.

(a) Explain the underlying rationale for algorithm/formulae;

(b) Use consistent variables, equation formats, subscripts, etc.;

(c) Number all equations;

(d) Define all parameters, coefficients, variables, etc used in the equations, with units indicated;

(e) Justify the conservativeness of the approach applied.

For each of the parameters, coefficients, variables, etc, the methodology shall describe the basis for the values to be selected for these variables.

(a) Where values are provided in the methodology:

   (i) Clearly indicate the precise references from which these values are taken (e.g. official statistics, IPCC Guidelines, commercial and scientific literature);

   (ii) Justify the conservative application of the values provided.

(b) Where values are to be provided by the project participant, the methodology shall clearly indicate how the values are to be selected and justified:

   (i) For variables that are not monitored throughout the project life time, but are derived from default values or one time measurements and remain fixed throughout crediting period, this shall be detailed in paragraph 8 of Section II;

   (ii) For variables that are monitored, this shall be detailed in paragraph 3 of Section III.

In the application of the methodology in the PDD for the ex ante estimation of the net anthropogenic

GHG removals by sinks over the selected crediting period, project participants may use reliable estimates for variables that are monitored and listed in paragraph 3 of Section III. However, if the methodology requires different approaches for the ex ante and ex post determination of actual net GHG removals by sinks, the methodology shall, in this section, clearly describe the differences between the ex ante and the ex post approaches and provide a consistent description of each approach, elaborating all algorithms, variables and formulae required. The Board has approved several A/R Methodological Tools. Please refer to the CDM website for these tools. The tools may be used whenever their applicability conditions allow. They should be used as stand-alone procedures, without changes, and need not to be copied but only referenced in the proposed methodology. Make sure that the applicability conditions of the tool are met by the proposed project activity, the carbon pools and emission source referred to in the proposed methodology corresponds to that in the tool, and that output of the tool and the methodology are consistent (e.g. with respect to units). Apart from using the existing approved tools, project proponents are also encouraged to propose new tools in areas where no tool exists or approved tools are not appropriate.

Explanation/justification (if not self-explanatory)

A/R WG assessment (to be completed by the A/R WG)

(a) Provide an assessment of the appropriateness and mathematical correctness of the methodological procedure to calculate actual net anthropogenic GHG removals by sinks. Explain any shortcomings and list the required changes. Include an assessment of:

(i) The choice of algorithms/formulae and/or models used and correctness of their application (e.g. mathematical deficiencies, inconsistencies in calculus of dimensions);

(ii) The appropriateness (adequacy, consistency, accuracy and reliability) of the parameters used in the methodology;

(iii) State, whether the procedure may lead to systematic overestimation of the actual net anthropogenic GHG removals by sinks, taking into account the uncertainties associated with the data and parameters used. Assess whether the procedure can be carried out in an unambiguous way, replicated, and subjected to a validation and/or verification study. Identify any shortcomings and list the required changes.

(b) State whether the approach/language applied by PPs follows to the maximum possible extent the one used in the approved A/R CDM methodologies and whether any differences reflect differences in the substance. If not, identify the inconsistencies.

6. Leakage

Methodology procedure

Explain whether any leakage sources have been excluded, and if so, justify their exclusion. Elaborate all algorithms and formulae used to estimate measure or calculate leakage. Be specific and complete, so that the procedure can be carried out in an unambiguous way, replicated, and subjected to a validation and/or verification study.

(a) Explain the underlying rationale for algorithm/formulae;

(b) Use consistent variables, equation formats, subscripts, etc.;

(c) Number all equations;

(d) Define all parameters, coefficients, variables, etc. used in the equations, with units indicated;

(e) Justify the conservativeness of the approach applied.

Explanation/justification (if not self-explanatory)

A/R WG assessment (to be completed by the A/R WG)

(a) State, whether the choice of leakage emission sources considered is appropriate. Indicate any important leakage emissions sources that have been neglected in the context of the applicability conditions;

(b) Provide an assessment of the appropriateness and mathematical correctness of the methodological procedure to calculate ex ante leakage emissions. Explain any shortcomings and list required changes;

(c) State whether the approach/language applied by PPs follows to the maximum possible extent the one used in the approved A/R CDM methodologies and whether any differences reflect differences in the substance. If not, identify the inconsistencies.

7. Net anthropogenic GHG removal by sinks

Methodology procedure

Elaborate all algorithms and formulae used to calculate net anthropogenic GHG removal by sinks. Be specific and complete, so that the procedure can be carried out in an unambiguous way, replicated, and subjected to a validation and/or verification study.

(a) Use consistent variables, equation formats, subscripts, etc.;

(b) Number all equations;

(c) Define all parameters, coefficients, variables used in the equations, etc, with units indicated;

Please provide for the formulae to calculate net anthropogenic GHG removals by sinks for project activities using tCERs and for those using lCERs. Please refer to the latest guidance by the Board regarding these formulae.

A/R WG assessment (to be completed by the A/R WG)

(a) Provide an assessment of the appropriateness and mathematical correctness of the methodological procedure to calculate ex ante actual net anthropogenic GHG removals by sinks. Explain any shortcomings and list the required changes;

(b) State whether the approach/language applied by PPs follows to the maximum possible extent the one used in the approved A/R CDM methodologies and whether any differences reflect differences in the substance. If not, identify the inconsistencies.

8. Data and parameters not monitored (default values used or possibly measured one time)

Data / Parameter:

Description/unit:

Source of Data

Measurement procedures

Monitoring frequency

QA/QC frequency

Any Comments:

A/R WG assessment (to be completed by the A/R WG)

State whether the compilation of data and parameters not monitored is complete, appropriate, and justified. Identify any shortcomings and list the required changes.

Section III : Monitoring Methodology

All data collected as part of monitoring should be archived electronically and be kept at least for two years after the end of the last crediting period. All measurements should be conducted according ton relevant standards, including the monitoring provisions contained in the tools referred to in this methodology.

1. Monitoring of project implementation

Methodology procedure

Provide a procedure to clearly identify and document the implementation of the project on the land areas within the project boundary including:

(a) The species, size, timing and geographical location of the stands established as part of the project activity;

(b) Whether the stands are managed according to any requirements defined in the methodology (e.g. to obey the applicability conditions);

(c) Where relevant: whether the applicability conditions still apply to the project activity.

Explanation/justification (if not self-explanatory)

A/R WG assessment (to be completed by the A/R WG)

Assess the appropriateness of the procedure to monitor and document the implementation of the project on land areas within project boundary. Explain any shortcomings and list the required changes.

2. Sampling design and stratification

Stratification of the project area into relatively homogeneous units can either increase the measuring precision without increasing the cost unduly, or reduce the cost without reducing measuring precision because of the lower variance within each homogeneous unit. PPs should present in the AR-CDM-PDD an ex ante stratification of the project area or justify the lack of it. The number and boundaries of the strata defined ex ante may change during the crediting period (ex post).

Methodology procedure

Describe how the sampling design is to be undertaken for the ex post calculation of actual net GHG removals by sinks and, in case the baseline is monitored, the baseline net GHG removals by sinks. The sampling design may, inter alia, include stratification, determination of number of plots, plot distribution, etc. The ex post stratification may be based on the ex ante stratification of the project area, in which case the methodology shall contain the steps for updating it, if required.

The sampling design may, inter alia, include information on size and shape of the plots for each carbon pool considered in the project activity, determination of number of plots and sample size calculation, plot distribution, etc. PPs may use the tool for .Calculation of the number of sample plots for measurements within A/R CDM project activities. For estimation of the number of permanent sample plots needed for monitoring changes in carbon pools at a desired precision level. (EB 31, Annex 15). Explain how the sampling design and the monitoring methodology achieve reliable estimates of net anthropogenic GHG removals by sinks.

Explanation/justification (if not self-explanatory)

A/R WG assessment (to be completed by the A/R WG)

Assess the appropriateness and correctness of the sampling design procedures for the ex post calculation of actual net GHG removals by sinks and determination of the ex post baseline net GHG removals by sinks (if required). The sampling design may include determination of number of plots, plot distribution, etc. Identify any shortcomings and list the required changes.

3. Data and parameters monitored

The following parameters should be monitored during the project activity. While applying the relevant equations provided in this methodology for the ex ante calculation of net anthropogenic GHG removals by sinks, PPs shall provide transparent estimations for the parameters that are monitored during the crediting period.

Data / Parameter:
Description/ unit:
Source of Data
Measurement procedures
Monitoring frequency
QA/QC frequency
Any Comments:

Note any parameters, coefficients, variables, etc. that are used to calculate baseline net GHG removals by sinks, actual net GHG removals by sinks and leakage where values are to be provided by the PPs and the parameters, coefficients, variables, etc, are monitored throughout the project life time. This may include data that is measured or sampled and data that is collected from other sources (e.g. official statistics, expert judgment, proprietary data, IPCC, commercial and scientific literature, etc.). Data that is calculated with equations provided in the methodology should not be included in the compilation. Use the tables provided in the CDM-NM to provide the following information for each parameter, coefficient or variable:

(a) Under data/parameter., the variable used in equations in the baseline methodology;

(b) Under Data Unit., use International System Units (SI units. refer to<http://www.bipm.fr/enus/3_SI/si.html)>;

(c) Under description, a clear and unambiguous description of the parameter;

(d) Under Used in equations, list the numbers of all equations where the variable is used;

(e) Under Measurement procedure and/or source of data., clearly indicate how the variables will be monitored. Provide:

    (i) A description of the measurement procedures or reference to appropriate standards. For data that is collected from other sources, indicate what types of sources are suitable (official statistics, expert judgment, proprietary data, IPCC, commercial and scientific literature, etc.);

    (ii) The vintage of data that is suitable;

(iii) What spatial level of data is suitable (local, regional, national, and international);

(iv) How conservativeness of the values is to be ensured.

(f) Under Monitoring frequency, a description of the frequency of monitoring (e.g. annually, etc);

(g) Under QA/QC procedures, a description of QA/AC procedures. For assumptions and measurement procedures that have significant uncertainty associated with them, include how such uncertainty is to be addressed.

A/R WG assessment (to be completed by the A/R WG)

State whether the compilation of data and parameters monitored is complete, appropriate, and justified. Identify any shortcomings and list the required changes.

4. Conservative approach and uncertainties

To help reduce uncertainties in the accounting of emissions and removals, this methodology uses whenever possible the proven methods from the GPG-LULUCF, GPG-2000, the IPCC Revised 2006 guidelines and tools and guidance approved by the Board on conservative estimation of emissions and removals.

It is recommended that PPs identify key parameters that would significantly influence the accuracy of estimates. Values that are specific to the project circumstances should be obtained for these key parameters, whenever possible. These values should be based on:

- Data from well-referenced peer-reviewed literature or other well-established published sources

- National inventory data or default data from IPCC literature that has, whenever possible and necessary, been checked for consistency against available local data specific to the project circumstances; or
- In the absence of the above sources of information, expert opinion may be used to assist with data selection. Experts will often provide a range of data, as well as a most probable value for the data. The rationale for selecting a particular data value should be briefly noted in the CDM-AR-PDD. For any data provided by experts, the CDM-AR-PDD shall also record the experts name, affiliation, and principal qualification as an expert (e.g. that they are a member of a country's national forest inventory technical advisory group). A one-page summary CV for each expert consulted should be included in an annex.

In choosing key parameters or making important assumptions based on information that is not specific to the project circumstances, such as the use of default data, PPs shall follow the most recent version of the Guidelines on conservative choice and application of default data in estimation of the net anthropogenic GHG removals by sinks.

Methodology procedure (if any)

Explanation/justification (if not self-explanatory)

A/R WG assessment (to be completed by the A/R WG) State, whether the methodology takes into account uncertainties by appropriate choice of monitoring methods, such as number of samples, to achieve reliable estimates of net anthropogenic greenhouse gas removals by sinks. State whether the methodology ensures that the net anthropogenic GHG removals by sinks are estimated in conservative manner, taking into account the uncertainties of the methodology. If not, identify the shortcomings and list the required changes.

5. References

A/R WG assessment (to be completed by the A/R WG): Assessment of the description and consistency of the methodology

(a) State whether the proposed A/R CDM methodology has been described in an adequate and transparent manner. If not, identify the shortcomings and list the required changes;

(b) State whether any other source of information (i.e. other than documentation on this proposed A/R methodology available on the UNFCCC CDM web site) has been used by you in evaluating this methodology. If so, please provide specific references;

(c) Indicate any further comments

References

Adams, D.M., R.J. Alig, B.A. McCarl, J.M. Callaway, and S.M. Winnett. (1999). "Minimum Cost Strategies for Sequestering Carbon in Forests." *Land Economics* 75: 360-74.

Blaser, J. and C. Robledo (2008). Initial analysis on the mitigation potential in the forestry sector. Update of a background paper prepared for the UNFCCC Secretariat in August 2007. Presented to the International Expert Meeting on Addressing Climate Change through Sustainable Management of Tropical Forests, Yokohama, Japan, 30 April–2 May 2008.

Eliasch, J. (2008). Climate change: Financing global forests. Office of Climate Change, UK.

FAO (2004). Carbon sequestration in Dryland soils. *World Soil Resources Reports* No. 102. pp 126.

FAO (2002). Harvesting carbon sequestration through land-use change: A way out of rural poverty? In: *The state of food and agriculture 2002.* Rome.

Fay, C., H. de Foresta, M. Sarait, and T.P. Tomich, (1998). A policy breakthrough for Indonesian farmers in the Krui damar agroforests. *Agroforestry Today*, 10(2), 25-26.

Garrity, D.P., Simons Tony, Verchot, L., and Swallow, B. (2008). Tackling climate change through agroforestry: A review of ICRAF's research agenda, current project and future opportunities. 23 January, 2008, World Agroforestry Center, Nairobi.

Garrity, D.P. (2009). Conservation agriculture and agroforestry in the context of environmental change" Paper presented in the 4th World Congress on Conservation Agriculture. 4-7 Feb. 2009, New Delhi, India.

Grieg-Gran, M. (2008). The Cost of Avoiding Deforestation: Update of the Report prepared for the Stern Review of the Economics of Climate Change. Working Paper. International Institute for Environment and Development. Cambridge, UK.

Houghton, R.A. (1999). The annual net flux of carbon to the atmosphere from changes in land use 1850–1990. *Tellus*. 51B: 298–313.

Houghton, R.A. (2003). Revised estimates of the annual net flux of carbon to the atmosphere from changes in land use and land management 1850–2000. *Tellus*. 55b: 378-390.

Intergovernmental Panel on Climate Change, (2007). Mitigation of Climate Change. Report of Working Group III. Cambridge: Cambridge University Press.

IPCC (2000). Special report on Landuse, Landuse Change and Forestry. Robert T. Watson, Ian R. Noble, Bert Bolin, N. H. Ravindranath, David J. Verardo and David J. Dokken (Eds.). Cambridge University Press, UK. pp 375.

IPCC (2001). Climate change. Mitigation. Bert Metz, Ogunlad Davidson, Robert Swart and Jiahua Pan (Eds). Cambridge University Press, UK. pp 700.

IPCC (2007). Working Group III Report on Mitigation of Climate Change. IPCC Fourth Assessment Report. Bert Metz, Ogunlade Davidson, Peter Bosch, Rutu Dave and Leo Meyer (Eds.) Cambridge University Press, UK. pp 841.

Kindermann, G., M. Obersteiner, B. Sohngen J. Sathaye, K. Andrasko, E. Rametsteiner, B. Schlamadinger, S. Wunder, R. Beach, (2008). "Global cost estimates of reducing carbon emissions through avoided deforestation." *Proceedings of the National Academy of Sciences.* 105(30): 10302–10307.

Lubowski, R., A. Plantinga, R. Stavins, (2006). Land-use change and carbon sinks: Econometric estimation of the carbon sequestration supply function. *Journal of Environmental Economics and Management.* 51: 135-152.

Murray, B., R. Lubowski, and B. Sohngen, (2009). Including International Forest Carbon Incentives in a United States Climate Policy: Understanding the Economics. Working Paper. Nicholas Institute for the Environmental Policy Solutions, Duke University.

Murray, B.C., B.L. Sohngen, A.J. Sommer, B.M. Depro, K.M. Jones, B.A. McCarl, D. Gillig, B. DeAngelo, and K. Andrasko, (2005). EPA-R-05-006. "Greenhouse Gas Mitigation Potential in U.S. Forestry and Agriculture." Washington, D.C: U.S. Environmental Protection Agency, Office of Atmospheric Programs.

Patnaik, R.K. and Sahoo, A.K. (2009). Adaptation of Agroforestry and Production Forestry in enhancing Carbon mitigation in India. *Environment & Ecology* 28(1):45-55.

Plantinga, A.J., T. Mauldin, and D.J. Miller, (1999). An Econometric Analysis of the Costs of Sequestering Carbon in Forests. *American Journal of Agricultural Economics* 81: 812-24.

Richards K. and C. Stokes, (2004). A Review of Forest Carbon Sequestration Cost Studies: A Dozen Years of Research. *Climatic Change.* 63: 1-48.

Roshetko, J.M., Lasco, R.D. and Angeles, M.S.D. (2006). Small holder Agroforestry Systems for Carbon Storage. Mitigation and Adaptation Strategies for Global Change. Springer. Publ.

Sahoo, A.K., Singh, A.K. and Patnaik, R.K. (2010). Reducing Emissions from Deforestation and Degradation: A New Framework for Improving Forests and livelihoods. *Journal of Tropical Forestry.* 26(IV), 13-17.

Sahoo, A.K. (2011). Climate Change and Forestry. The Text Book of Forest Ecology, Biodiversity and Conservation, IBD, Dehradun.

Sedjo, R.A. (1989). Forests: A Tool to Moderate Global Warming? *Environment* 31(1): 14-20.

Sedjo, R.A., J. Wisniewski, A.V. Sample, and J.D. Kinsman, (1995). The Economics of Managing Carbon via Forestry: Assessment of Existing Studies. *Environmental and Resource Economics* 6: 139-65.

Singh, V.P. (2008). Agroforestry for food, livelihoods and environmental security. Paper presented during the India- Africa Summit, 10-12 Nov. 2008, New Delhi, India.

Singh, V.P. (2009). Conservation agriculture and agroforestry in the context of equity and poverty elimination. Paper presented in the *4th World Congress on Conservation Agriculture*. 4-7 Feb. 2009, New Delhi, India.

Singh, A.K and Sahoo, A.K. (2011). Carbon Economics and Small holders Livelihood in India . *Environment and Ecology*. 29(2A):822-830.

Sohngen, B. and R. Mendelsohn (2003). An Optimal Control Model of Forest Carbon Sequestration. *American Journal of Agricultural Economics*. 85(2): 448-457.

Sohngen, B. and R. Mendelsohn, (2007). A Sensitivity Analysis of Carbon Sequestration. Chapter 19 in *Human-Induced Climate Change: An Interdisciplinary Assessment*. Edited by M. Schlesinger, H.S. Kheshgi, J. Smith, F.C. de la Chesnaye, J.M. Reilly, T. Wilson, and C. Kolstad. Cambridge: Cambridge University Press.

Sohngen, B., A. Golub, T. Hertel, (2009). The Role of Forestry in Carbon Sequestration in General Equilibrium Models. Chapter 11 in *Economic Analysis of Land Use in Global Climate Change Policy*. Edited by T. Hertel, S. Rose, R. Tol. New York: Routledge.

Stavins, R. The Costs of Carbon Sequestration: A Revealed Preference Approach, (1999). American Economic Review 89:994-1009.

UN Food and Agricultural Organization, (2006). Global Forest Resources Assessment 2005: Progress towards sustainable forest management. FAO Forestry Paper 147. United Nations Food and Agricultural Organization. Rome, Italy. www.fao.org

UNFCC (2008). Challenges and opportunities for mitigation in the agricultural sector Technical paper.

UNFCCC (1996). Technology inventory and assessment: Initial report on an inventory and assessment of technologies to mitigate and adapt to climate change. Subsidiary Body for Scientific and Technological Advice, Second session. Geneva, 27 February - 4 March 1996.

UNFCCC (2000). Methodological issues land-use, land-use change and forestry. Subsidiary Body for Scientific and Technological Advice Twelfth session Bonn, 12-16 June 2000.

UNFCCC (2008). Ad Hoc Working Group on Long-Term Co-operative Action under the convention. Fourth Session Poznan 1-10 December 2008.Ideas and submissions from intergovernmental organisations. Ideas and proposals on the elements contained in paragraph 1 of the Bali Action Plan. Paper No1 FAO and IFAD. *Financing climate change adaptation and mitigation in the agricultural and forestry sectors.*

UNFCCC, (2001). Report of the conference of the parties on its seventh session, held at marrakesh from 29 October to 10 November 2001. FCCC/CP/2001/13.

UNFCCC/CCNUCC, (2008). CDM Executive Board Report 37. Annexure 3; Procedures for the submission and consideration of a proposed new methodology (Version 13).

van Kooten, G. Cornelis, Alison J. Eagle, James Manley and Tara Smolak, (2004). How Costly are Carbon Offsets? A Meta-analysis of Carbon Forest Sinks, *Environmental Science & Policy* 7 (4 August): 239-51.

Verchot, L. (2006). Climate change in Africa:Agroforestry for adaptation and mitigation. *Paper presented in the Climate Change Forum.* 1-3 Nov. 2006, Nairobi, Kenya.

Verchot, L. (2007). Design and best practices for agroforestry and community forestry carbon projects: a workplan for ICRAF in the CPR Alliance. ICARF, Nairobi, Kenya.

Verchot, L. (2009). Carbon sequestration opportunities with smallholder communities: forest, agriculture and agro-forestry" Paper presented in the 4th *World Congress on Coservation Agriculture.* 4-7 Feb., 2009, New Delhi, India.

Index

MIX
Papier | Fördert gute Waldnutzung
FSC® C083411

Kolibri 360 GmbH
Ferdinand-Jühlke-Straße 7
99095 Erfurt, Deutschland
produktsicherheit@kolibri360.de